Management of Local Processors and Terminals

IT Infrastructure Library

Ivor J Macfarlane

Gildengate House,
Upper Green Lane,
NORWICH, NR3 1DW

London: HMSO

004.6RT

© Crown Copyright, 1992

Applications for reproduction should be made to HMSO

First published 1992

ISBN   0 11 330550 8

This is one of the books in the IT Infrastructure Library series. At regular intervals, further books will be published and the Library will be completed by early 1993. Since many customers would like to receive the IT Infrastructure Library books automatically on publication, a standing order service has been set up. For further details on standing orders please contact:

HMSO Publicity (P9D), FREEPOST,
Norwich, NR3 1BR
(*No stamp needed for UK customers*).

Until the whole Library is published, and subject to availability, draft copies of unpublished books may be obtained from CCTA if you are a standing order customer. To obtain drafts please contact:

IT Infrastructure Management Services
CCTA
Gildengate House, Upper Green Lane,
NORWICH, NR3 1DW.

For further information on other CCTA products, contact:

Press and Public Relations,
CCTA
Riverwalk House
157-161 Millbank
London SW1P 4RT.

This document has been produced using procedures conforming to
BS 5750 Part 1: 1987; ISO 9001: 1987.

Table of Contents

	Foreword	vii
1.	**Management Summary**	1
2.	**Introduction**	5
2.1	Purpose	5
2.2	Target readership	6
2.3	Scope	6
2.3.1	Scope of 'organization'	7
2.3.2	IT equipment outside IT directorate control	8
2.3.3	Definition of 'local processors'	8
2.3.4	Definition of 'terminal'	9
2.4	Related guidance	9
2.5	Standards	11
3.	**Planning for the management of local processors and terminals**	13
3.1	Procedures	13
3.1.1	Resources and responsibilities	14
3.1.2	Customer liaison	17
3.1.3	Help Desk	17
3.1.4	Service Level Agreements	18
3.1.5	Procurement policy	20
3.1.6	Support	24
3.1.7	Training	25
3.1.8	Configuration management	26
3.1.9	Capacity management	27
3.1.10	Software control and distribution	29
3.1.11	Installation, acceptance and testing	32
3.1.12	Cost management	34
3.1.13	Problem and change management	35
3.1.14	Maintenance considerations	35
3.1.15	Security	37
3.2	Dependencies	37
3.2.1	General dependencies	38
3.2.2	Technical constraints	39
3.3	People	39
3.3.1	Manager for Local Processors and Terminals (MLPT)	40
3.3.2	Local Systems Administrator (LSA)	40
3.4	Timing	42

4. Implementation — 45

4.1	Procedures	45
4.1.1	Resources and responsibilities	45
4.1.2	Customer awareness	46
4.1.3	Help Desk	46
4.1.4	Service level management	46
4.1.5	Procurement policy	46
4.1.6	Support	47
4.1.7	Training	47
4.1.8	Configuration management	48
4.1.9	Capacity management	48
4.1.10	Software control and distribution	48
4.1.11	Installation, acceptance and testing	48
4.1.12	Cost management	49
4.1.13	Problem and change management	49
4.1.14	Security	49
4.2	Dependencies	50
4.3	People	50
4.4	Timing	51

5. Post-implementation and audit — 53

5.1	Procedures	53
5.1.1	Resources and responsibilities	53
5.1.2	Metrics	54
5.1.3	Managing customer awareness	55
5.1.4	Help Desk	56
5.1.5	Service Level Agreements	57
5.1.6	Procurement policy	57
5.1.7	Support	58
5.1.8	Training	58
5.1.9	Configuration management	59
5.1.10	Capacity management	59
5.1.11	Software control and distribution	59
5.1.12	Installation, acceptance and testing	60
5.1.13	Cost management	60
5.1.14	Problem and change management	61
5.1.15	Security	61
5.1.16	Auditing of procedures	62
5.2	Dependencies	64
5.3	People	64
5.4	Timing	65

Table of contents

6.	**Benefits, costs and possible problems**	**67**
6.1	Benefits	67
6.2	Costs	68
6.3	Possible problems	69
7.	**Tools**	**71**
8.	**Bibliography**	**73**

Annexes

A.	**Glossary of Terms**	**A1**
	Acronyms and abbreviations used in this module	A1
	Definitions used in this module	A2
B.	**Example Service Level Agreement**	**B1**
B.1	Service Level Agreement - local network	B1
B.1.1	Example Service Level Agreement	B2
C.	**Acceptance, testing and installation**	**C1**
C.1	General considerations	C1
C.2	Technical acceptance standards	C1
C.2.1	Compatibility standards	C1
C.2.2	Installation standards	C3
C.3	Delivery considerations	C4
C.3.1	Delivery options	C5
C.3.2	Installation & checking of delivered items	C8
C.4	Example script for receipt, checking & installing a PC	C9
D.	**Skills and training required**	**D1**
D.1	Skills requirements	D1
D.2	Training requirements	D2
D.3	Rôle descriptions	D3
D.3.1	Manager with responsibility for local processors and terminals	D4
D.3.2	Local Systems Administrator	D5

IT Infrastructure Library
Management of Local Processors and Terminals

Foreword

Welcome to the IT Infrastructure Library module on the **Management of Local Processors and Terminals.**

In their respective areas the IT Infrastructure Library publications complement and provide more detail than the IS Guides.

The ethos behind the development of the IT Infrastructure Library is the recognition that organizations are becoming increasingly dependent on IT in order to satisfy their corporate aims and meet their business needs. This growing dependency leads to growing requirement for quality IT services. In this context quality means 'matched to business needs and user requirements as these evolve'.

This module is one of a series of codes of practice intended to facilitate the quality management of IT services and of the IT Infrastructure. (By IT Infrastructure, we mean organizations' computers and networks - hardware, software and computer related communications, upon which application systems and IT services are built and run). The codes of practice will assist organizations to provide quality IT services in the face of skill shortages, system complexity, rapid change, growing user expectations, current and future user requirements.

Underpinning the IT Infrastructure is the Environmental Infrastructure upon which it is built. Environmental topics are covered in separate sets of guides within the IT Infrastructure Library.

IT infrastructure management is a complex subject which for presentational and practical reasons has been broken down within the IT Infrastructure Library into a series of modules. A complete list of current and planned modules is available from the CCTA IT Infrastructure Management Services at the address given at the back of this module.

The structure of the module is, in essence:

* a **Management summary** aimed at senior managers (Directors of IT and above, typically down to Civil Service Grade 5), senior IT staff and, in some cases, users or office managers (typically Civil Service Grades 5 to 7)

* the main body of the text, aimed at IT middle management (typically grades 7 to HEO)

* technical detail in Annexes.

The module gives the main **guidance** in sections 3 to 5; explains the **benefits, costs and possible problems** in section 6, which may be of interest to senior staff; and provides information on **tools** (requirements and examples of real-life availability) in section 7.

CCTA is working with the IT industry to foster the development of software tools to underpin the guidance contained within the codes of practice (ie to make adherence to the module more practicable), and ultimately to automate functions.

If you have any comments on this or other modules, do please let us know. A **Comments sheet** is provided with every module. Alternatively you may wish to contact us directly using the reference point given in **Further information**.

Thank you. We hope you find this module useful.

Acknowledgements

The assistance of the following contributors is gratefully acknowledged.

Brian Mooney (under contract to CCTA from BIS Applied Systems);

PA Consultants (under contract to CCTA).

Section 1
Management summary

1. Management Summary

With the advent of ever more powerful personal computers and distributed IT systems, organizations are siting a greater proportion of their IT equipment within the business sections, rather than with the specialist IT function. This module of the IT Infrastructure Library addresses the practices and procedures necessary for establishing a co-ordinated approach across an organization to the use of IT equipment sited outside the IT directorate. Its guidance is designed to encourage consistent use of IT, bringing benefits in terms of interconnection and common language between the different business communities within that organization.

There is a strong feeling among business managers that IT is now too important to the success of the business to be left in the hands of the specialists. The increasing power of local processing brings with it increasing scope for processing to come under the control of local management. Centralized IT resources are still required, and will be for the foreseeable future, and whilst organizations can rightly look to their IT directorates to provide guidance, local management has an important rôle to play in the provision and management of IT resources in modern organizations.

This module of the IT Infrastructure Library gives guidance on establishing the best division of responsibilities between central (ie IT) and local (ie business) management for the provision of IT facilities within business areas. This is unlikely to be a simple task to achieve in any organization, but the benefits of doing it well are considerable:

* improved efficiency, effectiveness and economy across the organization

* consistency in approach throughout the organization

* the opportunity to get more output from staff and resources

* greater resilience in terms of hardware and staff skills

* reduced incidents and problems due to the adoption of a single approach throughout.

The inevitable corollary to these benefits is, of course, that by not recognizing the requirements of local processing, organizations (and business areas within an organization) will be left behind by their competitors in terms of ability to meet objectives.

The IT Infrastructure Library
Management of Local Processors and Terminals

The individual functions addressed by the IT Infrastructure Library are all applicable to the management of local processors and terminals, but care must be taken in applying them to the special circumstances of IT sited within business communities. This module examines those functions, highlighting the special circumstances relating to their application in this field. The IT directorate can provide vital support, especially in terms of procurement, training, professional advice and documentation, particularly through the development of corporate standards, without impinging on the benefits of moving day-to-day control of a local IT service to the business customers.

This module offers guidance in terms of practices and procedures including:

* identifying responsibility within the IT directorate for the co-ordination rôle by establishing a post with specific responsibility for local processors and terminals

* producing a manual documenting relevant information and guidance in a single place

* appointing Local Systems Administrators

* involving customers as much as possible in the planning of IT services and devolving responsibility for day to day control to business communities

* implementing the advice contained in the other volumes of the IT Infrastructure Library especially

    - service level agreements

    - software control and distribution.

The move of IT responsibility to business communities must not result in a dangerous weakening of security, especially as this move represents a potential increase in vulnerability to risk. Control of local processing is one of the key considerations in ensuring the confidentiality, integrity and availability of the data on the local equipment. This data is one of the organization's prime assets and should be recognized as such.

The introduction of corporate IT standards driven from the IT directorate will be perceived by many business managers as a threat to their authority. Achieving successful implementation is likely to require commitment at Chief Executive level if (as is likely) disputes over areas of responsibilities arise. Procrastination over the introduction

Section 1
Management summary

of a function to manage local processors and terminals will only serve to make the task even harder in the future, whilst the cost to the organization in terms of lost efficiency and effectiveness increases.

The drive for the introduction of a formal policy delineating responsibilities is likely to come from the IT directorate. However, in common with many other initiatives within IT service management, the benefits to the organization as a whole will largely be delivered by the business units' ability to perform in a more efficient, effective and economic fashion.

The IT Infrastructure Library
Management of Local Processors and Terminals

Section 2
Introduction

2. Introduction

Traditionally IT equipment and services were seen as the exclusive preserve of the IT directorate, with customers physically separated from all processing equipment. That situation has changed and much IT equipment is now housed in the customer domain, with customer departments having a degree of control over the equipment and the applications running on it. This proliferation has resulted in hardware and software of differing (often incompatible) types between (and within) business areas. With a growing trend towards organization-wide, and even inter-organization, IT infrastructures and the interworking of services on these infrastructures, it is important that the dispersed hardware and software is managed as part of the overall infrastructure.

Often customer departments are geographically remote from the IT services departments that support them. The IT directorate will need to liaise with several differently organized customer communities. The need to adapt to differently organized customer communities produces complications in the provision of a consistent and quality service, even where the separation of IT and business communities is only logical. The division of responsibilities for the management of local processors and terminals between dispersed customer departments and the central IT Services department must be clearly agreed. By co-ordinating their approach to the planning and control of all the services on the infrastructure, organizations will find themselves providing better services to the customer in a more cost-effective and efficient fashion.

2.1 Purpose

The purpose of this module is to provide guidance to assist organizations to manage local processors and/or terminals which are in the customer domain. In particular, the module offers advice to organizations' IT directorates on how to manage the IT infrastructure sited in the customer domain in a way that ensures efficiency and a smoothness of operation. This will enable:

* required service levels, as specified in Service Level Agreements (SLAs), to be met

* all information to be available to any part of the organization, as corporate need arises.

The IT Infrastructure Library
Management of Local Processors and Terminals

Organizations must develop an agreed working practice for managing the local IT infrastructure in a corporate fashion, in order to foster consistency and compatibility in both equipment and practices throughout the organization. Many organizations will, however, have business areas with needs which cannot be met within the 'standards based' approach and will therefore have to be treated as exceptions. A typical example would be a design department, where IT equipment with specific graphical requirements precludes the use of an organization's standard issue IT equipment.

Within the IT directorate, management responsibility for co-ordination and control of local IT must be established before agreed working practices can be developed and implemented.

2.2 Target readership

The module is aimed at IT Service Managers, and those IT managers with responsibility for the control of local processors, small computers or terminals, including Small System Group Managers and Information Centre Managers. The module will also be of relevance to the Help Desk Manager and in some organizations to the Network and/or the Computer Operations Manager.

Business managers whose staff use local processors or terminals may also find the module of use.

2.3 Scope

This module addresses the installation of hardware and software enhancements to an IT infrastructure within the customer domain. Installation of a major distributed system, eg downsizing from mainframe to PC based IT services, should be treated as a major project and falls outside the scope of this module.

IT infrastructure management functions are required to manage local processors and terminals effectively. They are, however, less easy to implement and review in the local processing environment than when applied solely to IT equipment within the computer centre.

The approach taken in sections 3, 4 and 5 is to take each relevant IT infrastructure management function in turn and examine its application to the management of local processing and terminals, making the division of management responsibility between IT staff and their customers and users clear.

Section 2
Introduction

Specifically, the document addresses the concept that, to manage local processors and terminals effectively, organizations have to:

* recognize that the IT infrastructure and associated services require active management, even when physically located in the customer domain

* develop procedures to

  - meet the needs of the organization, the IT directorate and its customers

  - ensure compliance with all applicable constraints

  - incorporate best business practice

  - maximize efficiency, effectiveness and economy

* implement the procedures

* monitor the procedures and adjust them to suit changing requirements.

2.3.1 Scope of 'organization'

Within this module, the word organization is used to refer to an entity with a single broad accountancy and management structure. A public sector organization might be a department or an executive agency; in the private sector a small autonomous company within a group or a multi-national concern. Within that entity, the staff responsible for providing IT services are referred to as the IT directorate. This may vary from a complex unit with several hundred staff to one person supporting a handful of PCs on a part-time basis.

This module has been written to provide guidance for internal IT directorates rather than an external IT service provider which would supply services on a contractual basis.

These externally provided services would normally (but not always) be managed through the IT directorate on behalf of customers. Inevitably, there will be situations which fall between the two clear cut scenarios, with quasi-independent organizations, relying on another organization for the provision of common services such as personnel, security and IT support.

2.3.2 IT equipment outside IT directorate control

Guidance is given on establishing a function to control, co-ordinate and support the use of IT equipment sited in the customer domain. Central control of IT equipment will not normally extend to IT equipment wholly financed, maintained and used by a single customer, except in so far as it is linked via networks to IT equipment and services elsewhere. However, the organization may choose, as a part of its IS strategy, to encourage users of such equipment to join in a corporate approach to IT, providing increased consistency, contingency and value for money throughout the organization. Where such overtures are resisted and no support or advice is sought from the IT directorate, it follows that no control or influence can be exerted over the way such equipment is used. Where customers have obtained IT equipment against the advice of the IT directorate, permission to connect that equipment to any centrally provided services is likely to be withheld.

2.3.3 Definition of 'local processors'

For the purpose of this module a 'local processor' is typically a Personal Computer (PC), but it could also be a mini-computer providing service exclusively to a single business area and sited within the customer domain. Although there will be a substantial element of customer management of the computer, some level of support and control of it will be provided by the IT directorate. Where IT expenditure for local processors is authorized against customers' budgets, it will be common for the central IT directorate to advise on the purchase of both hardware and software. This will often be done by way of an approved list of equipment and agreed organizational standards on connection, operating systems etc, helping to ensure consistency and compatibility throughout the organization.

Examples of local processors include:

* stand alone PCs with commercial software packages such as word processing and spreadsheets, used by individuals. Portable and transportable microcomputers are included

* a Local Area Network (LAN) server and any attached PCs distributed among one or more customer sections providing access to package software and/or in-house software

* mini-computers with distributed terminals providing computer support to a single section's business eg stock control across several warehouse locations

* any PC or communications equipment such as modems or multiplexors that are used to implement a Wide Area Network (WAN) to connect PCs and/or terminals providing both local processing facilities and access to central IT services.

2.3.4 Definition of 'terminal'

For the purpose of this module a terminal may be any device in the customer domain from which tasks can be initiated by customers to run on the organization's IT infrastructure located elsewhere.

Such terminals may be described as 'intelligent' (when they are a PC with terminal emulation) or 'dumb' when they have no other function besides accepting manual input and receiving responses.

Simple cabling between local processors and terminals is included in the scope, but external communications networks, such as switched telephone lines, corporate data networks and private circuits are excluded.

2.4 Related guidance

This module is one of a series that constitute the CCTA **IT Infrastructure Library**. Although the module can be read in isolation, it is recommended that it is used in conjunction with other modules.

It is important to bear in mind that the physical location of local processing does not alter the need for management, but it does imply that the functions described in the IT Infrastructure Library need to be modified when they are applied to the management of local processing and terminals. For example, specific IT expertise will still be required to solve local processing problems, but it may need to be partially devolved from central IT to the customer location for problems which require unique local knowledge. The following IT Infrastructure Library modules are therefore relevant.

Customer liaison

The **Customer Liaison** module describes the steps necessary for IT staff to ensure effective liaison is achieved with their customers. Customer liaison practices must be viewed as an essential cornerstone to all the guidance

The IT Infrastructure Library
Management of Local Processors and Terminals

provided in this module, since otherwise any management procedures impacting on the customer domain will be impossible to implement satisfactorily.

Help Desk, change, configuration and problem management
: The **Help Desk**, **Change Management**, **Configuration Management** and **Problem Management** modules describe the functions vital to the efficient and effective provision of an IT service on any size or configuration of IT equipment including local processors and terminals. These modules detail all that is required to implement and control those functions.

Network management
: The **Network Management** module describes the procedures necessary to plan and manage an efficient network. Local Processors and Terminals generally rely on an efficient network to function effectively.

Service level management
: The **Service Level Management** module recommends that wherever possible the provision of IT services should be documented in service level agreements. This recommendation applies equally to services running on local processors.

Software control and distribution
: Control of software in an IT infrastructure and its distribution to local processors is essential for efficient and effective service provision. The **Software Control and Distribution** module describes the procedures and practices required and the reasons for them.

Supplier relationships
: The **Managing Supplier Relationships** module describes the techniques needed to liaise effectively with suppliers concerning the supply and maintenance of equipment, software and services. Such liaison is an important aspect of the management of local processors and terminals, since the supply and maintenance is likely to take place away from the control of the IT directorate.

Third party and single source maintenance
: The **Third Party and Single Source Maintenance** module covers the benefits, problems and procedures associated with single source maintenance, which has particular advantages for the maintenance of local processors.

Cost management
: The **Cost Management** module covers the apportionment of IT costs and charging back to customer departments for the provision of IT services. It is especially likely in the provision of local processing to customers that there will be a requirement for any centrally incurred costs, eg support, to be distributed equally to the various customers.

Section 2
Introduction

Testing software for operational use	The **Testing Software for Operational Use** module gives guidance on ensuring that software and documentation relating to additions or changes to an IT infrastructure are adequately tested before being used in the live environment. Comprehensive testing is particularly difficult in the multiplicity of combinations and circumstances presented by the widespread use of IT throughout an organization.
Contingency planning	Adequate contingency back up is essential for all IT services of whatever size. The **Contingency Planning** module gives full detail on appropriate procedures, most of which are relevant to local processors. The opportunities for transferring work between machines in a disaster situation are often significant when working with small distributed IT equipment.
Capacity management	Guidance is given in the **Capacity Management** module on the matching of capacity and demands for computer systems, networks and local processors.
Cable infrastructure strategy	**Cable Infrastructure Strategy** considers the strategic issues, costs and benefits of planning, installing and maintaining the cabling vital to the efficient functioning of local processing equipment.
Office environment set	The following modules from the Office Environment set of the IT Infrastructure Library contain detailed information essential for any manager with responsibility for local processors and terminals:

* **The Office Working Environment and IT**
* **Managing a Quality Working Environment for IT**
* **Office Design and Planning**.

2.5 Standards

Standards applying directly to local processors and terminals are not yet mature enough to provide a stable platform on which to base an organization's long term future plans. However, standards on the interoperability concepts of open systems should be considered and applied wherever possible. The introduction of a standard approach within an organization, and with its trading partners etc, will lead to benefits from electronic transfer, compatibility and consistency of approach.

BS7179 - Ergonomics of Design and Use of Visual Display Terminals (VDTs) in Offices. (to be subsumed in ISO9241)

BS7179 provides recommendations to promote health and safety considerations for working with display screen equipment. Minimum requirements are defined in European Directive 90/270/EEC and will be the subject of regulations in the Health and Safety at Work etc Act. IT staff with responsibility for managing the provision and use of local processors and terminals should be familiar with these standards and directives.

ISO9001/EN2900/BS5750 - Quality Management and Quality Assurance Standards.

The IT Infrastructure Library modules are being designed to assist adherents to obtain third-party quality certification to ISO9001. Organizations' IT directorates may wish to be so certified and CCTA will in future recommend that Facilities Management providers are also certified, by a third-party certification body, to ISO9000. Such third-parties should be accredited by the NACCB, the National Accreditation Council for Certification Bodies.

Section 3
Planning for the management of local processors and terminals

3. Planning for the management of local processors and terminals

The planning section of this module addresses the need for, and practicalities of, the management of local processing. The aim is to retain a corporate approach to IT processing without unnecessary restrictions on the development of local solutions to local problems.

Locally sited IT equipment has become more powerful and more popular in recent years. In many organizations, such equipment has been allowed to proliferate in response to locally perceived needs, with no single plan to ensure consistency of approach or avoid expensive repetition of mistakes and little consideration of future requirements, either local or corporate.

IT processing in organizations is moving away rapidly from the traditional concentration in a central facility and this move to local and distributed processing seems set to accelerate in the future. Managers with responsibility for ensuring the efficient and effective use of local and distributed processing are therefore under increasing pressure within organizations.

The establishment of a function within the IT directorate to manage the use of local IT infrastructure helps to prevent problems occurring in the future due to lack of co-ordination and control. The environment to be addressed is necessarily complicated, spanning as it does the various business units of an organization, and the function must be flexible enough to address with equal validity all the differing demands arising from the range of business units to be supported.

3.1 Procedures

The planning process is vital to the successful introduction of the function. Such plans must be realistic and agreed by all the parties involved before any implementation begins.

A first step in producing viable plans to implement this function, is to recognize the need for agreed working practices to be applied to local processors and terminals. To be beneficial these agreed working practices must have the support of IT managers and support staff as well as their customers. This section of the module advises on the elements to be considered in drawing up agreed working practices and planning for their implementation.

The IT Infrastructure Library
Management of Local Processors and Terminals

3.1.1 Resources and responsibilities

The first stage of the planning process is to establish the resources to be managed, and where the responsibilities lie. These resources include:

* hardware
* staff, both IT and business
* software
* documentation.

.1 Organizational structure

To assist in establishing a function to carry out the necessary degree of central control over IT infrastructure in the customer domain, the IT Services Manager must set up an organizational structure to divide management responsibility between customers and IT directorate.

IT Service Managers must identify, within their staff resources, responsibility for the function of managing local processors and terminals. Whether this is a full time post, or is combined with other IT service management responsibilities, will depend on:

* the size, complexity and geographical distribution of the organization
* the IT skills present in the business areas
* the present and expected promulgation of IT in the customer domain
* where (geographically) the support rôle will be located - with customers or with central IT services.

It should be realized that this is a rôle taken on by someone within the IT Services organization, it should not be viewed as an additional resource; in many organizations the responsibilities associated with this rôle will previously have been distributed across many posts. Concentrating them in one post will facilitate the introduction of central control and co-ordination over the use of local IT equipment throughout an organization. For convenience this rôle will be referred to as the Manager for Local Processors and Terminals (MLPT) throughout the rest of this book.

Section 3
Planning for the management of local processors and terminals

Initially the MLPT will carry out the following planning tasks in close co-operation with Local System Administrators (LSAs), see 3.3, and the other IT Service Managers. It is recommended that, especially where little or no formal management of local processing exists in an organization, a formal project is instigated to introduce management of local processors and terminals. CCTA recommends the use of the PRINCE project management method for controlling such projects.

.2 **Determine current situation**

Where a comprehensive and accurate Configuration Management Database (CMDB) exists, this is able to supply details of the hardware, software, networks and documentation in use throughout the organization. Even where such a CMDB is maintained, it is worth carrying out an audit to establish the scope of its coverage since, typically, the least likely parts of an IT infrastructure to be accurately recorded are:

* software used on PCs (checking whether the software and packages actually resident coincides with authorized records)
* equipment used for home working
* pooled or shared equipment where no single individual is willing to take responsibility
* low value equipment
* equipment likely to be enhanced or reconfigured locally.

These are the very elements of the IT infrastructure forming the MLPT's responsibility.

Since configuration management of all IT equipment remains the responsibility of the configuration management function, such an audit is technically their responsibility, rather than an aspect of the management of local processors and terminals. The MLPT, however, is the person most likely to ensure that the CMDB is kept up to date through auditing of local equipment.

It is at least equally important that the quality and quantity of existing support to customers is determined. This is, necessarily, a more subjective assessment. If a Customer Liaison function exists within the IT directorate then their

The IT Infrastructure Library
Management of Local Processors and Terminals

assistance should be sought. An accurate picture of how the IT directorate is perceived by its customers is vital if planning for the introduction of a new function is to be successful.

This picture is an essential and vital part of the planning process for the introduction of a function to manage local processors and terminals. If customers, especially at the management level, are not involved and encouraged at the earliest stage then it is unlikely that they will, in later stages, be willing to provide the support essential to the successful implementation of the function.

.3 **Division of responsibilities**

Although most IT infrastructure management functions are relevant to the management of local processors and terminals, their implementation will depend upon:

* the current culture of the organization

* the size of the organization and the number of remote units (logically and geographically).

The first step in establishing the current situation is to catalogue the existing services. It is then necessary to evaluate all these factors and plan, in conjunction with the respective IT service manager, the introduction of each IT infrastructure management function and the division of management responsibilities that is required.

The rest of this section highlights the IT infrastructure management functions that need to be planned and the recommended division of responsibilities.

.4 **Identify required changes**

An analysis of the current situation will lead to an identification of the changes required in order to achieve the desired function to manage local processors and terminals.

Metrics should be identified and incorporated in the planning where possible to describe quantitatively the effectiveness of the MLPT function. Appropriate metrics would address the areas of:

* availability of IT services to customers

* response of Help Desk to MLPT-based incidents

Section 3
Planning for the management of local processors and terminals

* customer satisfaction, determined from surveys
* expenditure and resources commitment on MLPT-related functions.

3.1.2 Customer liaison

The IT directorate's responsibilities in managing local processing will involve liaison with the management structure of most (if not all) the business areas in an organization. To ensure that this results in an efficient and effective service provision, good liaison with customers is of even more importance to the MLPT than the provision of central IT services.

There are several mechanisms that can be used to promote customer awareness of IT services:

* awareness campaigns aimed at customers
* presentations, targeted at specific business functions within the organization, where problems might be anticipated
* meetings with interested parties
* production of newsletters
* initiation of user groups for customer staff throughout the organization
* training in relevant skills.

Planning for effective customer communications is covered in the **Customer Liaison** module of the IT Infrastructure Library.

3.1.3 Help Desk

The Help Desk is the single point of contact with the IT directorate for all customers. A good Help Desk enables rapid resolution of problems and enable customers to continue working effectively. In dealing with incidents relating to local processors and terminals, Help Desk staff make use of the local knowledge and IT experience of the LSAs to enable more accurate diagnosis after the initial customer contact. Many organizations choose to route requests from customers to the Help Desk via the LSA. This offers the advantage of:

* amalgamating several reports of a similar incident which affects customers in a single location
* filtering out trivial faults

* dealing with local problems in situ, making use of local knowledge, both geographically and of practices and procedures within a specific business unit

* allowing LSAs to visit the customer's workplace to identify the cause of the incident

* building up customer's familiarity with, and confidence in, the LSA.

It is essential that LSAs report to the Help Desk all incidents reported to them, even if they have been solved locally. Unless this is done statistics and management information produced will not be accurate nor facilitate proactive problem solving. The Help Desk manager must be aware of local attitudes and must not allow a strong minded LSA to block any customer's access to the Help Desk facility.

The **Help Desk** module covers in detail the steps involved in setting up a Help Desk and the procedures required to run it effectively, including the provision of local and/or specialist Help Desks, designed to deal with discrete or specialist areas of the organization's IT usage.

3.1.4 Service Level Agreements

The IT Infrastructure Library **Service Level Management** (SLM) module covers the introduction and monitoring of service level agreements (SLAs). There are however some additional considerations to take into account when introducing SLAs into the local processing environment. Particularly in simple cases, the full rigour expounded in the SLM module is not appropriate and a reduced version is preferable.

The higher the IT proficiency and self-sufficiency of the customer department, the greater is their control over the performance of their own IT services. Such proficiency and potential autonomy is to be encouraged because:

* it frees central IT resources for more constructive and productive effort

* it makes customer departments more likely to use the equipment effectively and responsibly if they feel it is 'theirs to control'

* customers with a high degree of IT skills inevitably try to take over the day-to-day running; attempts to fight this tendency may cause needless friction and mutual distrust for no constructive benefit.

Section 3
Planning for the management of local processors and terminals

In encouraging this autonomy, the MLPT, together with the Service Level Manager, should encourage the adoption of SLAs within the customer community for the provision of IT services. Typically SLAs which are internal to a business community will be simple and restricted in their scope. They serve, however, as an important tool in providing and monitoring IT services. In agreeing service levels and workloads, they provide a firm and reliable basis for forward planning, clearly identifying the responsibilities of both IT provider and customer. An example of such an SLA is provided in Annex B.

To maximize local processing resource availability the following may be considered for inclusion in SLAs relating to local processing equipment:

* the use of fallback hardware such as spare PCs and terminals held locally
* contingency processing or communications facilities eg mirror-disk processors, dial-up lines in addition to leased lines
* fault tolerant processors/storage devices
* emergency generators
* Uninterruptible Power Supplies (UPS).

In many circumstances, the LSA acts in a local co-ordination rôle for services which are supplied by the IT directorate. In this situation an SLA is between the IT directorate and the customers, with the LSA adopting the responsibility for monitoring (and perhaps negotiating) the SLA on behalf of the customers. Formal acceptance of the SLA should be made at the highest practicable management level to emphasize that the business sector as a whole accepts the terms of the agreement.

Alternatively some of the agreements may be internal to the customer domain, where computing facilities are controlled by local staff on a day to day basis, eg a departmental mini-computer operated by customer staff or services based upon a LAN administered by an LSA. In this situation any SLA is between the LSA and the local customers. Any services provided by the central IT service in support of the local IT provision should be viewed as underpinning support and be subject to a separate agreement between the IT directorate and the LSA.

The IT Infrastructure Library
Management of Local Processors and Terminals

Whilst in many situations the rôle of the LSA is readily identified as falling clearly into one of the categories described, there are occasions when the situation is seen as falling between the two. If in doubt, and given that the LSA is under the management control of the customer, then any agreement should be established between the IT directorate and the customer.

The Service Level Manager should ensure that all customers (especially LSAs and business managers) are fully aware of the benefits of SLAs. The Service Level Manager provides support and guidance directly to any customer site where needed, liaising with the MLPT as appropriate. It may prove practical to assign an audit responsibility to the IT directorate (Service Level Manager and/or MLPT) for all agreements produced between local providers and customers of an IT service.

3.1.5 Procurement policy

Procurement policy should address the provision of a common set of procedures to a diverse set of business customers. The IT directorate should formulate a preferred list of hardware and software for the different types of use they envisage within the installation.

Government organizations should take account of the relevant obligations under EC/GATT legislation, namely the Supplies Directives as implemented in the UK by the Public Supply Contracts Regulations 1991, and the EC Decision on IT Standards, 87/95/EEC which covers the use of standards in procurement specifications. Preferred lists will be formulated taking account of advertisement and competition requirements under the same EC/GATT legislation.

The policy should define:

* levels of responsibility for approval of requests

* procurement schemes (bulk purchase arrangements and purchase timing considerations which may be linked to inventory levels)

* preferred hardware suppliers

* agreed set of machine profiles for different classes of need eg local PC, network PC, processing engine, file server

* supported operating systems

* a preferred set of supported application software

Section 3
Planning for the management of local processors and terminals

* a generalized set-up to which machines should be installed

* operational standards for the use of machines, including

    - documentation requirements

    - backup and archiving requirements

    - security and encryption

* a set of standard and tailored training which is offered to support the approved hardware and software. This might include

    - instruction manuals

    - approved courses

    - self-teach software

    - training videos

* procedures for procuring hardware and software outside the scope of the policy and the implications of so doing.

The procurement policy should provide a framework for the provision of local IT equipment and related software for the organization, irrespective of where the actual buying decisions are carried out.

All procurement for IT requirements should be reported to the IT directorate, irrespective of policy on buying decisions, to enable:

* actual IT spend and policy to be monitored, and if necessary co-ordinated to make best use of corporate buying power

* performance of suppliers to agreed contracts to be monitored

* call off against contracts to be monitored.

In considering requests for IT procurement, the approval body (this may be the business manger or within the IT directorate) should take into account whether:

* the case has been justified by

    - need/benefits

    - cost saving

- current policy

* the requested IT provision falls within the procurement policy guidelines

* the impact on existing services has been identified and is acceptable; eg network server load and output requirements

* there are adjustments to maintenance agreements required to include the procured kit.

The policy will change over time as requirements and available IT services evolve. The policy must contain a revision mechanism. This mechanism should also be used to consider requests for equipment which fall outside the standards. In reviewing requests for non-standard equipment, a decision must be made as to whether the request:

* falls outside the scope of the policy as a recognizable exception

* requires the policy to be amended to include a new category

* can be fulfilled by provision of equipment within the standard

* will not proceed.

It is important that procedures are designed and actioned in such a way that allows a repeated procurement to be communicated to interested parties at an early stage, at an appropriate level of detail, and any concerns aired as soon as possible. It may be useful for the IT directorate to circulate as examples the best constructed business cases. LSAs should, when required, use their IT expertise to help customer groups compile business cases.

Once procurement is successfully completed, IT staff should ensure that issues relating to the support and training of new customers as well as equipment installation and acceptance testing are undertaken by the necessary IT Services section so that the customers are smoothly guided through the introduction of their new IT equipment.

Procedures should include provision for the auditing of completed procurements, in accordance with any quality management system in place.

Section 3
Planning for the management of local processors and terminals

Suitability of service level agreement (SLA)

It may be useful to make some or all of the stages of procurement subject to an SLA. The areas relevant for inclusion include:

* lead times for
    - setting up initial discussion between customers and IT staff
    - feasibility investigation
    - technical and financial approval
    - obtaining information from vendors on non-standard products
    - supplying products and services against approved orders
* holding of internal stocks of equipment and consumables.

The incorporation of these aspects of the relationship between customers and the IT directorate into a formal SLA can provide the following benefits:

* a clear framework for both customers and the IT directorate to plan within
* comprehensive documentation detailing the rôle of each party in the procurement process
* appropriate levels of stockholding, saving tied up capital and floor space.

When agreeing SLAs, the following factors, which will affect the level of service that can be provided, should be borne in mind:

* projected pattern demand for services from customers, identifying any known cycles, peaks and troughs in the workload
* staff availability, and the effect of
    - leave, including allowances for sickness
    - other work commitments
* overall IT workload resourcing and priorities
* any other dependencies
    - industrial relations consultation framework
    - organizational policies and procedures.

The IT Infrastructure Library
Management of Local Processors and Terminals

Requests for procurement should be classified both in terms of priority (perceived value to the organization) and urgency (customers desire to meet a particular ready-for-service date) at an early stage. This will avoid unnecessary pressure and help to achieve an efficient deployment of resources.

The establishment of a mutually agreed grading system will help to clarify the situation for all staff involved.

3.1.6 Support

The degree of involvement of IT staff in the running of local processors will vary between organizations and across different sites in a single organization, but some degree of specialist technical support will invariably be required by those responsible for equipment in the customer domain.

To be able to provide guidance on the most effective support framework, the MLPT must first identify the customers' requirements for local processing. Account should be taken of the likely hours of usage, number of users, location and skill levels of the customer population, and the degree of local self-sufficiency that can be achieved.

The MLPT must also be able to identify how customer needs fit in with overall IT support policies and priorities. This task is an essential pre-requisite to drawing up SLAs.

LITES manual

The MLPT will produce a manual of guidance for customers using local processors and/or terminals. This guidance, constituting a 'Local IT Equipment and Services (LITES) manual will cover the basic principles for making best use of IT services within the organization. This manual should be a controlled document, issued in an easily updated form (eg loose leaf binder). To be of value, the manual must be:

* kept up to date
* written in everyday language, with a glossary of common IT terms
* restricted to relevant information.

Among other items, the manual should include:

* instruction on initial access to IT services through local equipment
* security procedures

Section 3
Planning for the management of local processors and terminals

- * procedures for cleaning and minor maintenance
- * Help Desk/LSA contact points, including out of hours contacts
- * catalogue of services available
- * procedure for ordering consumables.

Depending on the type and complexity of services, equipment and customer, other items may usefully be included. The content, frequency of update and format should be developed with customers, involving:

- * managers within the customer base
- * end-users (ensure those involved reflect the ability range of the user population, if the guide is to be of use it must be easily understood by all customers)
- * Local Systems Administrators(LSAs)
- * relevant IT services managers, including Service Level and Help Desk Managers.

3.1.7 Training

The MLPT should arrange product specific training as needed, maintaining a record of appropriate training course availability, including assessments from staff who have attended such courses.

With large implementations or less familiar technology it may be beneficial to test out training methods and courses before committing the organization to using that course (or training method) throughout. Following a first running, the achievements should be assessed against the training requirements and any changes identified brought to the attention of the providers (who may be the IT directorate).

If training is to be carried out on-site, it may be necessary to make computer resources available. The planning processes should therefore include consultation with all relevant parties.

Training requests should be routed back to the respective LSA after an initial Help Desk contact since:

- * customers may be new to the technology or services and could have several problems which require experience rather than skill to solve

* customers may be unskilled and likely to need frequent assistance at a basic level

* several customers are likely to be affected by a single problem

* customers are likely to require training that is related to their own departmental work patterns and data.

3.1.8 Configuration management

Configuration management is both an important and difficult function to introduce and administer. The greater the distribution of the IT equipment and the more responsibility for it rests upon customers, then the greater the difficulty and importance of configuration management. Recent surveys suggest that the biggest security problem faced by Government IT directorates was the theft of PCs and other small IT equipment. As an absolute minimum organizations require an asset management system that records movement of equipment in and out of buildings.

The introduction of a new function to co-ordinate and control local processors and terminals should include an audit of the hardware, software and documentation throughout the organization. Unless full configuration management is in existence, then there is liable to be a considerable discrepancy between records and reality. Time and resources expended on an audit are necessary and beneficial, since, otherwise, subsequent work is likely to be based upon false data and therefore likely to produce proposals which are not appropriate to the organization's actual situation.

In a small organization it may be possible to maintain a central CMDB of local processing and terminal equipment that is updated on a regular basis, by the Help Desk sending out the current configuration owned by the customer and asking for any amendments to be listed.

In larger organizations this approach can break down. The number of PCs, laptops and peripherals that move location can make configuration management impracticable through a centrally maintained CMDB.

Consequently, a single conceptual CMDB, built from the data contained in local records maintained by the LSA is likely to be more effective. The LSA can update the database

Section 3
Planning for the management of local processors and terminals

and could even personally control the movements of portable equipment. Under this approach a global CMDB is produced automatically by software that collates all individual CMDBs. The data may be uploaded to form a single actual CMDB or merely accessed by the Management Information System (MIS) software as shown in figure 1, overleaf.

The IT Infrastructure Library **Configuration Management** module gives detailed advice on determining the level of configuration items (CIs), the content of the CMDB and all aspects of configuration management.

Procedures must be developed to ensure all relevant staff are made aware of:

* new equipment being brought into service
* equipment being taken out of service, due to
    - irreparable failure
    - disposal due to redundancy
    - damage or theft
* movement of equipment between customers and/or locations.

These procedures must take account of the organization's security practices, particularly where equipment is being disposed of after having been used to store sensitive or classified data.

3.1.9 Capacity management

The IT Infrastructure Library **Capacity Management** module contains brief guidance on the applicability of capacity planning techniques to stand alone and networked PCs. The task is not straightforward since PCs rarely provide adequate monitoring. Monitoring information and capacity planning is likely to be feasible on mini-computers providing support to larger business communities and is also becoming available for Unix-based IT services. Guidance in the Capacity Management module is directly applicable in those circumstances.

The IT Infrastructure Library
Management of Local Processors and Terminals

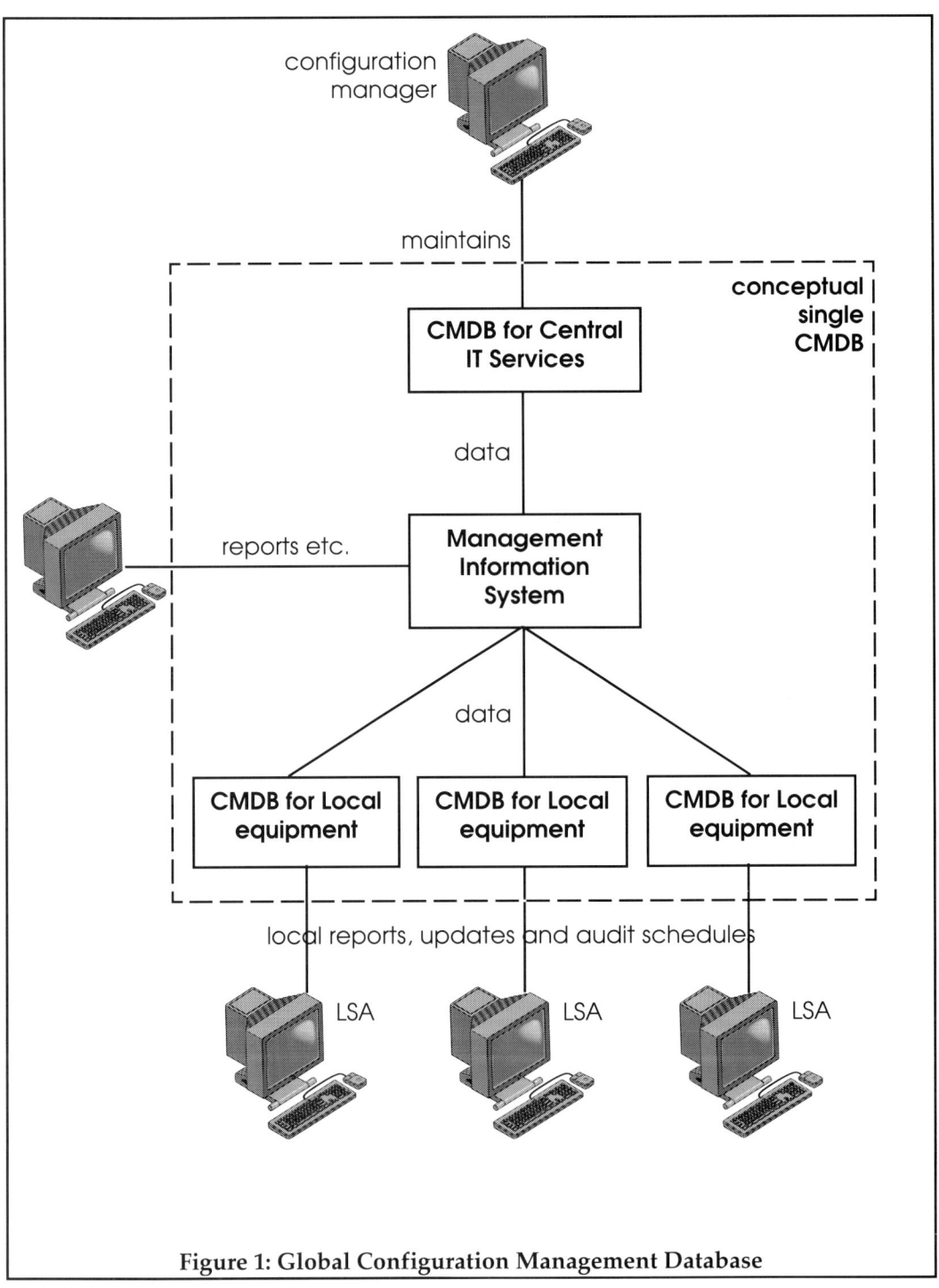

Figure 1: Global Configuration Management Database

Section 3
Planning for the management of local processors and terminals

For PC-based IT services, capacity measurement and planning based upon that measurement is generally restricted to:

* disk utilization; snapshots of disk utilization can be obtained, especially in conjunction with

    - software updates (see 3.1.10)

    - configuration management audits (although if such audits are advertised in advance, the amount of programs and data resident on PCs may well be lower than during unannounced audits!)

* network usage and response times over LANs

* requests for additional equipment.

3.1.10 Software control and distribution

The proper control and distribution of software can best be exercised where formal configuration management is in place.

In the distributed environment of local processing, control over the distribution of software is essential to ensure consistency. If formal configuration management is not practised, an accurate and up-to-date asset register of all PCs detailing the software authorized to be on each machine is essential. Such control and authorization will lead to less risk of malicious software, such as viruses, entering IT systems. Without a precise knowledge of what should be where, consistency, throughout the organization and associated efficiency and effectiveness, is impossible.

Whatever mechanisms are used to distribute software, customers must be made aware of the timing of any changes, any consequences of the changes as far as their work is concerned and any fallback contingencies that will be available if problems arise.

Software Control and Distribution is part of configuration management. The distribution of new software and documentation to customers using locally based IT should be arranged by the Configuration Manager in co-ordination with the MLPT.

Where there is a large number of PCs in an organization, the distribution and installation of new, enhanced or changed software can be a difficult task to achieve effectively. This is especially true where not all the PCs are identically configured. The most efficient solution to the problem is to automate the task as far as possible.

.1 **Automating software distribution**

There are two discrete aspects to the distribution of software viz:

* the preparation of a mailing list detailing which computers require updating with a new software release. This will not necessarily be the same for every software release, but may vary according to the authorized software on each machine

* the technique used for distributing and implementing the software release.

There is considerable scope for automation of both aspects. The stages of progress towards complete automation of each aspect can be summarised:

* in producing the mailing list

    - paper based mailing list produced by reference to inventory

    - paper based list generated electronically from CMDB

    - update media appropriate to each PC produced by software, taking data automatically from database

    - appropriate update despatched automatically to customers

* distributing the software release by

    - direct installation by LSAs or MLPT staff visiting each PC

    - direct installation from supplied media by Configuration Management staff

    - direct installation from supplied media by customers

    - software controlled updating by use of batch tasks resident on supplied media

    - software controlled updating via network.

Section 3
Planning for the management of local processors and terminals

The further that progress is made along the two strands of automation, the more effective the task of software control and distribution to local processors should be. The efficiency is also likely to increase provided the software is reliable. It must be borne in mind that the type of software required to drive automatic updates over a large network, to a complex mix of differently configured PCs, is notoriously difficult to test. Specifically, accurate replication of a complex network in a safe test environment is prohibitively expensive and testing on the live network is liable to cause significant disruption to customers. It is therefore essential that a detailed and realistic costing of potential benefits and an analysis of the associated risks be carried out before embarking on the development of such software.

Distribution of software changes via a network can, of course, only function comprehensively where *every* piece of local processing equipment is attached to the network. Where some equipment is not attached, two distribution procedures will have to function in parallel, which can increase the chance of oversight or error.

.2 **Confirmation of update**

However the software change is achieved, a confirmation mechanism must be incorporated into the method. Without this confirmation the IT directorate can have no confidence that all customers are working with the correct release of software at any given time. For direct installation this may be in the form of an authorized signature on a record sheet. Where the software update is carried out by a software driven automated task, the confirmation is equally important. In this case the confirmation would consist of either:

* the customer (or automation software) returning a confirmation message over the network, or

* by the customer returning the floppy disk containing the software controlling the update, with a confirmation message having been written to it as part of the updating procedure.

Some software changes must be introduced at a precise time, eg changes to tax tables, new price ranges or pay scales. In this situation trigger times can be built into the updating software to allow distribution and confirmation of successful installation to take place in advance of the time of bringing into service.

The IT Infrastructure Library
Management of Local Processors and Terminals

.3 **Software audit at update**

The installation of new or changed software by the LSA onto a PC can be used as an opportunity to carry out several checks on the PC and to report back to the IT directorate. Among the investigations possible by using automated software are:

* detection of unauthorized software eg

    - old versions of software

    - known viruses

    - pirate copies of software authorized for use on other PCs within the organization

    - known undesirable games

* analysis of disk utilization

* data checks

* confirmation of all previous relevant software changes being made.

3.1.11 Installation, acceptance and testing

When new equipment is to be installed into a customer site, IT Services need to determine, monitor and control potential problems during the initial installation and acceptance testing phases. The MLPT must take responsibility for ensuring that any changes to the customer's working environment proceed smoothly and without undue disruption.

Local equipment is likely to be under the day-to-day control of customers. For this reason it is vital that customers are involved in establishing installation and acceptance policy in the earliest stages of acquisition. In particular customers must be involved in developing and carrying out the testing of supplied hardware, software and documentation. To be cost effective such testing must reflect the perceived risk of failure. Since this risk depends heavily on the importance of the supported business function, customer staff are uniquely positioned to assess it accurately. The validation and verification of documentation is often overlooked by IT staff. Since for the most part such documentation is aimed at end-users with minimal IT skills these are the best people

Section 3
Planning for the management of local processors and terminals

to test its fitness for purpose. The IT Infrastructure Library **Testing Software for Operational Use** module covers these concepts in greater detail.

Local IT facilities can be very powerful, complex and vital to the organization's business. It is common for the products of many different suppliers to be incorporated into a single system. Installation and acceptance testing must be properly planned by the IT directorate and followed through to ensure that the equipment purchased is carrying out the functions for which it was obtained.

Procedures

Procedures also need to be put in place for establishing local installation standards, and individually tailorable options, such as help screens available with application software. Controls are required to co-ordinate the provision of new facilities to customers with the necessary support and training activities.

The Configuration Manager will be responsible for recording an item as a CI on the CMDB on notification that it has been ordered. When the item has been received, the status of the CI will be amended to reflect that it has been accepted, tested and installed. Procedures must be developed to ensure that the Configuration Manager is informed of the current status of all such CIs.

Inform customers

The Help Desk must ensure that all customers affected by the installation and acceptance testing are informed of timescales and any events requiring attention, devoting particular attention to new customers, stressing that the Help Desk will attempt to resolve all incidents.

Where customers are unfamiliar with new concepts, the acceptance of elements of IT can be unsuccessful. The MLPT should arrange for training on appropriate IT issues to introduce concepts gradually and successfully.

Installation

Installation as a result of agreed changes will take place in accordance with the change management procedures.

Some installations, especially those that require re-cabling or new flooring, can be extremely disruptive to a customer's working environment and the IT directorate must minimize inconvenience. It is critically important that customers are involved in the agreement of disruption times during installation and acceptance testing.

The installation of local equipment should be co-ordinated as appropriate with Premises, Facilities and/or Network Managers. The change management system will include the advising of all involved staff as part of its routine procedures. However, detailed timing and liaison over changes may well be delegated by the change management function to MLPT, LSA, or project implementation staff.

All new workstations (including replacements for existing equipment) must comply with the relevant health and safety legislation, requiring a workstation analysis to be carried out.

Annex C covers the detailed considerations pertaining to the installation of IT equipment into the customer domain. It also covers the important aspects concerned with the physical installation of equipment into a customer site, discussing the pros and cons of IT staff being present for such installations. Potential exists for automating the installation of standard components, eg PCs, package software.

Installation sign-off criteria must be determined, such as:

* acceptance criteria, in terms of performance against pre-agreed tests

* a suitably defined period of successful operation, to a specified standard of performance.

Checklists or installation scripts are of benefit in helping to ensure that all staff carry out installation and acceptance procedures in a uniform fashion.

Testing facilities

Effective testing may require the provision of considerable ancillary equipment and accommodation as well as involving inevitable disruption to the customer location and business during final trialling. Customers must therefore be consulted about the provision of resources and the timing of such tests.

3.1.12 Cost management

As organizations increasingly require detailed breakdown of their IT costs, more and more organizations are appointing Cost Managers within their IT directorates.

The MLPT is likely to need to work closely with the Cost Manager in assisting with the allocation of costs and the preparation of any charging procedures applied to the provision of local processing.

The responsibility for such costing and charging will always remain with the IT Cost Manager, with the MLPT responsible for furnishing the information on which the costs (and charges) are founded.

Section 3
Planning for the management of local processors and terminals

3.1.13 Problem and change management

The IT Infrastructure Library **Problem Management** and **Change Management** modules cover in full detail the steps involved in setting up these functions and the procedures required in running them effectively. These procedures apply equally to local processors and terminals, although the following additional points should be borne in mind:

* all changes to local IT services (including hardware, software and documentation) should be agreed with appropriate LSAs as well as the Change Advisory Board (CAB) where central IT services are affected

* small changes (such as a PC move) should be under the control of the LSA with the necessary liaison with the Help Desk.

Requests for changes (RFC) should go via the change management system. In some organizations, the Help Desk as part of their customer liaison rôle may formally input changes initiated by customers. Each stage of the change, from request through authorization to scheduling for implementation is documented by configuration management. Forthcoming and implemented changes are notified to the Help Desk.

The installation of new hardware, software etc must be authorized by change management staff within IT Services for a time convenient to customers and IT staff. Equipment installed in the customer domain should be formally signed-off by the staff member responsible, as designated by the change management function. This is likely to be:

* the LSA (for installation of equipment and/or software at a remote location)

* the MLPT for changes to software or new projects.

A procedure must be developed by which local staff are informed in advance by LSAs of expected installation, relocation and disposal of IT equipment within their work area.

3.1.14 Maintenance considerations

Since IT equipment is often repaired on site, it is inevitable that customers or LSAs will have to deal with field service engineers when faults occur. Where local staff are authorized to report faults directly to the maintainers or repairers, these incidents should also be logged with the Help Desk. It is unlikely, however, that there will always be a representative of the IT directorate (or the LSA) present at the actual work site during the repair. Appropriate advice will always be available via the Help Desk.

Incidents concerning IT hardware are often resolved by the use of locally held spares; procedures should be devised by the MLPT and put in place to ensure the maintenance of any suitable stocks of appropriate PC spares at all times.

The adoption of a standardized configuration for an organization's PCs allows the economical retention of spare PCs. These would then be rapidly available to meet new requirements or to replace faulty equipment.

To ensure consistency, standard paperwork that the maintainer (whether external or in-house) can use as reference material must be kept available with each item of local processing equipment and each terminal. Much of the necessary information may be available from configuration management. The following items (where appropriate) should be included:

* specification details eg

    - model type and serial number

    - modifications record

    - communications interface specifications

    - equipment configuration data (eg required settings for DIP switch and software controlled options)

    - software required (eg for restarts)

* note of conditions to be supplied to all contractors' staff working on the site, this to include

    - adherence to change management and problem management procedures

    - maintenance contract details

    - restrictions on the removal of parts, especially hard disk drives, from the site

    - contact points in the IT directorate

    - on site security information

    - other useful domestic information eg canteen facilities, car parking, access arrangements

* incident recording paperwork to permit recording of
  - incident type and date/time of occurrence
  - time maintenance staff arrived and left
  - field engineer's comment, detailing all work done and signature.

3.1.15 Security

Security is an increasingly vital function in IT owing to the growing use of computing in all business functions. Locally based IT services are at risk from undesirable disclosure, modification, denial of service, or destruction which could have major repercussions, either financially or in terms of political or business impact.

Local processors in an office environment, including those which form part of distributed processing systems, are vulnerable to a wide variety of risks. Theft, viruses and insider hacking present some of the most significant threats to local processors, therefore putting sensitive data and the continued functioning of the business at risk.

The IT Security Officer should be consulted regarding risk assessment.

It is the responsibility of management at all levels to ensure that the IT services they are responsible for are appropriately secured at every stage of their life-cycle, from proposal through to disposal. IT management should satisfy themselves that local staff responsibilities are allocated to cover the routine security functions such as data backups, scheduled maintenance and fire precautions. Confirmation should be sought that there are sufficient back up personnel to carry out the functions adequately during holiday periods or during sick absence of usual staff.

New or changed equipment, software and/or business practices may well bring a need for changes to security arrangements, of which all involved staff must be made aware. The IT Security Officer can advise on any necessary revised arrangements and, in collaboration with IT services staff, initiate them via the change management system.

3.2 Dependencies

A successful function to manage local processors and terminals will require approval and acceptance of the plans at the very highest level of the organization. There must be commitment to the function at Chief Executive level, ie at a level of authority above the individual business areas. Without this level of support it will prove difficult to prevent the business communities determining their own individual approaches to local IT, reflecting their individual practices and priorities.

3.2.1 General dependencies

The planning process depends upon the established practices of the organization's business. In particular the framework for the management of local processors and terminals will be derived from, and must be consistent with, the organization's declared IS strategy and the organization's procurement policy. In practice these policies may well ease the planning process by providing a quality management system (QMS) within which the development of procedures for managing local processors and terminals can evolve.

Other influences upon the planning process will include:

* the current status of the organization, whether it is a 'greenfield' site with no IT infrastructure in the customer domain or whether the organization has IT that is currently being controlled and managed by customer divisions

* the physical size of the organization, the number of remote sites and their geographical distribution

* the abilities of the people charged with liaising with the IT customers including

    - communication skills, particularly in the persuasion of customers to adopt new, more formal procedures

    - technical knowledge of the IT equipment and services involved

    - knowledge of the particular business functions carried out by the various customer communities

* the history of IT development at the organization and in particular of the customer liaison function

* industrial relations agreements on demarcation or allowances

* the customer's skills, experience and attitude to the use of IT

Section 3
Planning for the management of local processors and terminals

* the customer's view of the IT directorate and the service that they provide.

The degree of authority devolved to customers will greatly affect the planning process. The greater the degree of control retained within the IT directorate, the more control can be exercised also over the planning process. Consideration must also be taken of relevant financial constraints, especially in ensuring that control for aspects of local processors and terminals are vested in managers with the financial authority to exercise that control.

Where the IT directorate is planning the establishment of a function to control and co-ordinate IT infrastructure in the customer domain, some degree of customer resistance is inevitable. This will especially be the case where customer departments have traditionally been free to procure and use IT without restriction. Any new initiative could be viewed as an erosion of local autonomy and this is only likely to be assuaged by tangible benefits in return.

3.2.2 Technical constraints

If a local processing system is not entirely self-contained, agreements are required for interfacing with other IT facilities, such as a network or mainframe equipment. Local processors and terminals need to comply with:

* agreed standards to enable connection to these facilities

* organizational policies on preferred equipment type, software standards and common practices, security and testing practices.

Where these standards and policies are not in existence, plans need to be prepared to develop them during the introduction of the function to manage local processors and terminals.

3.3 People

The successful management of local processors and terminals involves staff from all the business communities within an organization as well as from the IT directorate and other supporting services. In order to co-ordinate all those involved and obtain the necessary consensus views requires good communication and negotiation skills.

The IT Infrastructure Library
Management of Local Processors and Terminals

3.3.1 Manager for Local Processors and Terminals (MLPT)

The MLPT will need to act as the bridge between the central IT directorate (of which the MLPT is a part) and the business communities who own and control the IT systems and services on a day to day basis. The MLPT will be responsible for technical management of LSAs, and this will require careful liaison with the line managers of the LSAs within the business communities. Paramount among the skills required to perform the job well are:

* ability to see the requirements of the business communities in the context of their operational situation, not just from an IT standpoint

* up-to-date knowledge of the facilities and techniques available in the IT fields used within the organization

* appreciation of the need for compromise in achieving the best working patterns achievable in the various circumstances likely to be encountered across a diverse organization.

3.3.2 Local Systems Administrator (LSA)

To overcome the problem of managing IT in several customer areas (whether separated geographically or merely logically by organizational structure), LSAs are used. LSAs will typically be responsible to local management, particularly where the IT services support a single business unit. If there is a danger of competition and disagreement between business units sharing local resources, it may prove better for LSAs to be directly responsible to the IT directorate. Local agreements on resource sharing, allowing the LSA to provide the best service would be preferable; in any case there is a technical management responsibility on the IT directorate for the performance of the LSA. The number of LSAs required at each site depends upon:

* the number of customers at the site
* the amount and complexity of customer-based IT
* the level of IT literacy at the site.

Section 3
Planning for the management of local processors and terminals

With the facilities now available for the remote administration of IT systems, it is possible to develop a balance between the expertise which needs to be provided locally and that which can be supplied remotely from the IT directorate. Such a balance will depend upon specific consideration within an organization including:

* type of equipment used and remote facilities available

* geographical separation

* expected frequency of direct support being required

* security levels required, both for physical access and data protection

* business criticality and availability requirements of the IT services involved.

The LSAs are essentially the 'eyes and ears' of the IT directorate. They allow customer liaison and technical practices to be managed at the centre and implemented locally. The MLPT must ensure that LSAs are always kept up-to-date with events occurring in other parts of the organization (not just within the IT directorate). To this end it is often beneficial to bring all the LSAs together in a forum from time to time to ensure that they are presenting a consistent and up-to-date image and service. The frequency of these meetings would typically be once or twice per year, but might be higher where there is considerable change to IT services or business practices.

Skills required

Care should be taken when selecting LSAs. These people need to be able to cope with:

* disseminating IT news and information to customers

* administering customer systems where necessary for backups and the application of software updates

* providing guidance to customers on change control requests and perhaps presenting them in an accurate specification to the IT directorate

* helping to diagnose faults after initial Help Desk contact by, for example, checking local communications equipment

* verifying customer procurement requests to ensure that they are reasonable

* advising IT management about any problematic area at the site or any issue of particular annoyance to the customers involved.

This mix of skills will not always be available, but people with good interpersonal skills who can understand the likely problems will often be 'accepted' by the customers more quickly than those who appear remote and introvert.

A major problem faced by many LSAs will be the need to work to two disparate management structures, viz:

* local management, comprising the customers of the IT service within the supported business function

* IT management (usually the MLPT), responsible for technical control of the IT equipment.

Balancing the conflicts which may arise between these two groups will call for a considerable degree of diplomacy, since in most cases the LSA will need to be viewed by both parties as sympathetic to their views and understanding of their problems.

Annex D gives more detailed checklists of skills and training required for IT support staff.

3.4 Timing

The planning of IT initiatives should be seen as aiming to improve the operation of the business.

Timescales for planning the management of local processors and terminals will depend upon:

* whether the function is being imposed onto an existing situation or being prepared for a greenfield site

* the geographical distribution of equipment and/or staff, both customer and IT

* the degree of co-operation and enthusiasm from customers.

Where an initiative for managing local processors and terminals is taking place within an organization, much will depend on the procedures previously in place and how great a change in responsibilities is being planned. If the intention is to bring a large number of local processors, presently dealt with autonomously by customers, under central co-ordinated IT directorate control, then there is inevitably going to be customer resistance; due in part at

Section 3
Planning for the management of local processors and terminals

least to business managers feeling that their authority is being eroded. Realistic timetabling is then essential to take account of customers who, while they may be convinced of the benefits of local IT equipment over a long timescale, prove to be intransigent if attempts are made to hurry any transfer of responsibility.

Timetabling should be agreed by both parties involved to ensure a smooth transition to maximize the operational effectiveness. Due attention should be given to the transfer of skills, product knowledge and documentation.

The duration of the planning process is dependent to a great extent upon the degree of co-operation present between MLPT and customer managers. With full co-operation, even for a large organization with several hundred PCs and terminals, it should be possible to reach agreement within six months. When there is a need to bring in senior management to arbitrate, it would be more sensible to allow more time.

The IT Infrastructure Library
Management of Local Processors and Terminals

Section 4
Implementation

4. Implementation

Except in the rare instance of a greenfield site, the implementation of a new or revised IT function to manage local processors and terminals will have a noticeable effect upon management responsibilities throughout the organization, within and outside the IT directorate.

Customers, IT staff and management must have confidence in the plans and be supportive if the planned benefits are to be realized. Customers will have been involved in all stages of the decision making process, as should the IT staff whose jobs may be affected, eg Help Desk personnel.

4.1 Procedures

Broadly, the implementation phase of the project involves executing the plans previously agreed. If the plans have been carefully constructed it is likely that the major concerns during the implementation phase will be related to people. There is always, however, some need for plans to be amended in the light of reality and it is important that such changes are made with the agreement (or at the very least knowledge) of all those affected, involved or interested.

4.1.1 Resources and responsibilities

The Manager for Local Processors and Terminals (MLPT) should ensure that all staff are fully aware of their responsibilities and that any necessary training has been given. Staff accountabilities should be well publicized, including the responsibilities of:

* IT Services staff
* LSAs
* customers
* local IT security officer.

Arrangements to provide cover for these responsibilities due to staff absence should be made clear and job definitions agreed. Necessary training and familiarization commensurate with operational responsibilities should be given.

The IT Infrastructure Library
Management of Local Processors and Terminals

4.1.2 Customer awareness

Feedback from the MLPT's customer awareness campaign should be analyzed and acted upon. The opportunity exists to identify potential problems early and to avoid them by (minor) amendments to the plans controlling the implementation of the function.

In order to keep all staff informed of progress and possible changes to plans, the awareness campaign should be supplemented, as appropriate, by follow-up meetings, workshops, and the issue of circulars and newsletters.

The MLPT must also ensure that Trades Unions, and any other appropriate staff representatives, are consulted in sufficient time to take due regard of their observation and comment.

4.1.3 Help Desk

MLPTs should communicate to all IT staff and customers:

* hours when the Help Desk is manned by personnel and times when cover is provided by answerphone or emergency call out

* any local arrangements such as customers being required to liaise through a local administrator or co-ordinator.

They should also ensure that Help Desk staff are informed of 'second line' support arrangements ie problem management responsibilities and of cover for absence.

4.1.4 Service level management

It is recommended that a pilot Service Level Agreement (SLA) is implemented if all the supporting processes are in place from the start of the new management approach to local processors and terminals. If the supporting processes are to be phased then a pilot SLA should be deferred.

4.1.5 Procurement policy

The MLPT must ensure that documentation and/or presentations have covered:

* recommended products/standards (for government organizations, these will have been selected and specified in accordance with the relevant EC/GATT obligations)

Section 4
Implementation

* forms and paperwork required
* approval procedures, where the IT directorate have sign-off rights over local procurement
* configuration management interface
* the registration and storage of delivered items
* security requirements.

The procurement of IT may affect several business and IT functions, and will need to be undertaken in a way which is compliant with international obligations in respect of procurement procedures and the use of standards in technical specifications. All parts of the organization which may be affected by the procurement must therefore be kept informed of progress.

4.1.6 Support

Product specific documentation, together with procedural documentation, should be made available to customers by the IT directorate, for instance:

* standards for data entry
* keyboard templates
* *aide-memoires*, such as reference cards
* office procedures
* availability timings and backup requirements.

Ensure that the LITES manual has been distributed to all customer areas.

LSAs should ensure that customers are given suitable reminders before any scheduled events that will affect availability, such as backups.

The MLPT should also ensure that all points of contact for support are communicated and, if any products in use cannot be supported, this must also be made clear.

4.1.7 Training

Training in new procedures for both IT staff and customers should be finalized by the IT directorate, and feedback obtained to ensure that such training has been effective.

The IT Infrastructure Library
Management of Local Processors and Terminals

4.1.8 Configuration management

The MLPT must ensure that all existing configurations of customer IT equipment are accurately reflected on the CMDB. Where LSAs have responsibility for maintaining local CM databases, they must ensure that the data is accurate and complete.

The MLPT should remind customers of the importance of configuration management to the business and that the unaccounted *ad-hoc* movement of peripherals and PC equipment is unacceptable.

4.1.9 Capacity management

Capacity management of existing equipment in the customer domain is usually difficult since equipment is often shared. Capacity requirements cannot be predicted for many general purpose PC packages; disk capacity cannot be monitored without disrupting the customer's work.

4.1.10 Software control and distribution

The mechanics of implementing software upgrades on IT equipment at the customer sites will depend on the availability of any automated tools, but the MLPT should ensure that any customer procedures required to facilitate upgrades are distributed to all customers.

Checks should be made to ensure that all appropriate software tools are properly installed and licensed. Particular attention should be paid to the installation of the PC-based component of tools designed to communicate between the central IT processor and several remotely sited PCs.

Extra care is needed with the first release of new software following the introduction of new procedures. It is worth considering following the first release with a software audit as soon as possible.

4.1.11 Installation, acceptance and testing

New procedures for installing, accepting and testing IT infrastructure items in the customer domain are unlikely to cause problems during the implementation of new management procedures, since changes to the infrastructure

Section 4
Implementation

will logically be kept to a minimum at this time. It may prove beneficial, therefore, to ensure that these procedures are understood by staff, by means of awareness seminars and newsletters, in order to unearth potential problems at the earliest possible stage. MLPT staff may feel it safest to supervise the first attempt by local staff to carry out installation, acceptance and testing of newly installed equipment, to ensure that local staff have understood any new procedures.

4.1.12 Cost management

The IT directorate must ensure that all the planned cost management activities are implemented consistently across customer sites.

MLPT and LSAs should keep detailed records of all expenditure and staff time allocations during any support and training effort.

4.1.13 Problem and change management

The MLPT should ensure that all problem and change management procedures are communicated as necessary to their own staff, LSAs and customers.

Change management procedures should ensure that the Help Desk is informed for onward communication to customers of any changes that might affect the availability or response of their IT services, and to prevent Help Desk staff being unnecessarily inundated with calls.

Problems and changes will inevitably arise while implementing the MLPT function. These problems and changes will serve as an initial trial of the procedures.

4.1.14 Security

The local IT Security Officer should monitor security awareness and devise campaigns to improve particular aspects of security, including carrying out spot checks and security audits. Senior IT staff and customer managers should be made aware of their responsibility to provide commitment and visible backing to reinforce the messages.

Data Protection Act registrations should be made, where appropriate, for new services and checked for existing ones.

The IT Infrastructure Library
Management of Local Processors and Terminals

4.2 Dependencies

Before implementation of any revised management procedures takes effect checks must be made to ensure sufficient staff resources, accommodation and time are available to complete the process. Natural predispositions towards optimism in task scheduling should be guarded against, with realistic timescales produced for all stages of the implementation process. In addition, all necessary documentation must have been finalized and training of staff and customers carried out before the project is finally signed-off.

Any software tools identified as necessary must be installed, tested and accepted. Other possible dependencies include:

* relocation of staff
* preparation of new accommodation and/or facilities.

It is likely that there will be a degree of local resistance from customers to the implementation of new management practices and responsibilities. Where this is the case it is possible that customer department's business priorities may prevent (often at short notice) the expected resources being made available to smooth the changes. Time should be set aside for the MLPT and their staff to establish the level of co-operation at implementation time, both the degree of co-operation needed for successful implementation of the plans, and the degree of co-operation likely to be found in practice. It is essential that customers understand and co-operate in the new management function and therefore if adequate resources and staff commitment is not identified at this stage, then the project should be re-planned accordingly.

There may be dependencies on the existing central IT service management functions and agreement will be required on their rôles and on how interfacing will work.

4.3 People

The introduction of the function to manage local processors and terminals will improve the IT service provided to the organization as a whole, even though some people may lose a degree of local autonomy. Some of the senior business managers may refuse to take seriously directives issued by the IT directorate. The adoption of the practices described in this book should therefore be formally endorsed by the Chief Executive of the organization. It is important to try

Section 4
Implementation

and engender in all staff a feeling of enthusiastic co-operation by encouragement and education. If this approach fails, the function will have to be imposed, making the implementation and management considerably more difficult. If co-operation is not obtained, then the project is unlikely to deliver the benefits expected.

For any proposed changes to be brought in successfully, every person involved, (especially managers) must believe that there are realizable benefits for themselves as well as for the organization as a whole. IT staff must ensure that enough time is spent at the implementation stage with all affected people to ensure their interest and support is achieved and maintained. Many changes in procedure fail because insufficient time and effort is spent in persuading affected staff that what is going to happen will be of direct benefit to them. If possible, assurances from personnel department of job security, career prospects etc should be obtained.

Introduction of the MLPT function will impact on a greater number of staff than the implementation of other IT Infrastructure Management functions; furthermore those most affected are the customers of the IT directorate. If the project is not well handled, the reputation of the whole IT directorate will suffer.

It is likely that senior business customers will seek opportunities to retain responsibility for their own IT equipment. Questioning IT directorate's competence to take over that responsibility will be one of the methods adopted. The implementation of the MLPT function must therefore be handled carefully, with due regard for the pitfalls and with the expectation of opposition. The directors of IT and the business communities will have to be involved personally in ensuring the function's success, seeking feedback and maintaining the awareness of senior customers of the IT directorate and the senior management of the organization.

4.4 Timing

Implementation activities will need to be carried out in line with customer priorities, commitments and resource availability.

Specifically it will increase the chances of success if this function is not implemented in parallel with other changes to the organization. Periods of high time-critical work (eg end of financial year) should be avoided.

The IT Infrastructure Library
Management of Local Processors and Terminals

5. Post-implementation and audit

This section deals with reviewing the efficiency and effectiveness of new procedures following their implementation and the ongoing operation of those procedures.

5.1 Procedures

Once the basic procedures for managing local processors and terminals are in place, the rôle of the IT service manager responsible, ie the Manager for Local Processors and Terminals (MLPT), is to ensure that the infrastructure continues to function effectively and efficiently and to provide the required quality services in the face of changing needs. The MLPT must review the operation of the function and take any required follow up action by liaising with the other IT Service managers. A change management process must operate to ensure changes to the infrastructure and procedures are installed as required.

The business world does not remain static and it is important to review procedures, IT infrastructure and services, both in terms of continued relevance and effectiveness in satisfying the organization's needs.

The metrics identified at the planning phase (see 3.1.1.4) will be an indication of the success (or failure) of the implementation. Additionally consideration must be given to establishing more subjective assessment of the project's success such as acceptance of the function by customers.

5.1.1 Resources and responsibilities

There should be a review of the effectiveness of IT staff charged with IT Services responsibilities, and their feedback on workload and any difficulties sought. The MLPT should identify opportunities to help customers achieve greater self-sufficiency in the running of their local services. The review should establish whether a good split of responsibilities has been achieved between:

* IT directorate and its customers
* central IT and local support.

Demarcations and cover arrangements within the IT directorate should also be reviewed periodically. This is particularly relevant due to the trend towards greater functionality in local processing equipment and the enhanced ability of such equipment to interwork. Any appropriate revisions identified, such as updating job definitions, should be implemented.

The degree of involvement of the IT directorate in the management and day to day support of local IT services must be subject to frequent and regular review. There are several causes of and opportunities for the level of involvement to reduce, including:

* increasing expertise in running IT services among non-specialist staff as

    - modern equipment requiring less human involvement is introduced

    - IT services settle down into a routine workload following initial teething troubles at implementation

    - the IT related skills of non-specialist staff increase; especially as younger staff, familiar with IT in their education, are appointed to positions of responsibility

* scope for increased automation in

    - routine operations such as start up, close down and backup

    - exception handling and reporting

    - invocation of stand-by and alternative working following failures

* tendency to view small items of IT as genuine office equipment, with the consequent transfer of procurement and maintenance responsibility to senior customers

* formal IT costing/charging systems demonstrating the (usually high) cost of using skilled IT staff to carry out routine day to day management tasks in an area of low technical and/or business risk.

5.1.2 Metrics

Whoever is accountable for IT operations within the customer domain (LSA, customer or the IT directorate), some form of measurement must be taken to gauge the management effectiveness. As a corollary, measurement

Section 5
Post-implementation and audit

should only be taken in the context of a clear organizational objective; never as an end in itself. It should always be the case that the value of the collected data justifies the cost of collection.

Practicality of measurement

Measurements may be quantitative or qualitative. Discrete quantities, such as a cost, time intervals, or the number of incident reports will be objectively measurable; however, parameters such as user satisfaction, or system security are less easily definable, and it may be necessary to agree metrics more subjectively.

IT is an integral part of an organization's business equipment and this is particularly true in the case of local processing facilities where the PCs, printers etc are as much a part of the office environment as telephones and photocopiers. It is therefore often impossible to derive metrics which will measure only the contribution or efficiency of the IT aspects alone involved in a complex business operation.

This is not to say that metrics which relate to the whole business function are not in themselves useful. In many cases the ability to measure the effectiveness of the sum total of resources, human, building and equipment is of more constructive use to customer managers than any metrics which attempt to isolate an activity embedded in the normal operation of the organization.

5.1.3 Managing customer awareness

Periodic reviews will identify the level of success of the MLPT function, both in educating customers, and in getting the latter to retain information and act upon guidance. Such reviews will:

* analyze customers' queries (ie Help Desk calls relating to local processing)

* interview customers to test IT awareness, use of procedures etc

* audit local data maintained by users.

The MLPT will need to vary the methods used to communicate with customers (and the content of these communications), as the latter become more knowledgeable. MLPT staff should seek to update their knowledge of the customer community through informal visits and personal contact.

55

The IT Infrastructure Library
Management of Local Processors and Terminals

MLPT staff should aim to update their knowledge of new products and legislation applicable to local processing and so be able to provide the most effective support to customers. This knowledge should be used both to publicize customer successes in utilizing local IT services, and to prevent any recorded difficulties from recurring.

5.1.4 Help Desk

The interface between the Help Desk and LSAs should be regularly reviewed. The audit of sample incidents, interviewing Help Desk staff, LSA and customer will help to determine whether the interface between customer and Help Desk via the LSA is working smoothly.

The Help Desk will produce regular management information on the performance of the support service in general. Aspects with particular relevance to the management of local processors and terminals include:

* comparison of service at different customer sites and/or in different business units

* availability and reliability of different kinds/makes of IT equipment used throughout the organization

* number of calls logged by each LSA

* percentage of incidents resolved by the LSA before logging

* the average time taken to fix a hardware fault by the different maintenance companies operating, at different locations and on the different makes of equipment.

Particular attention should be paid to LSAs logging considerably less than the average number of calls. It is likely that there will be areas where LSAs are resolving incidents locally without recording them, leading to:

* inaccurate management statistics

* underlying trends behind a series of incidents remaining unrecognized

* local training needs not being met.

Any feedback received by the IT directorate from customers should be communicated to the Help Desk. Where it is likely to be beneficial, meetings between customers and Help Desk (management and operators) could be arranged in an effort to improve procedures.

Section 5
Post-implementation and audit

5.1.5 Service Level Agreements

All relevant SLAs should be reviewed regularly by the Service Level Manager to ensure that they continue to reflect business requirements. Appropriate review periods will have been written into such agreements, however if significant changes have been made to the business, IT directorate, equipment or service provided, SLAs should be reviewed immediately, rather than waiting for the next formal review to fall due.

If agreed targets are not being met, remedial action should be put in hand. Specifically, SLAs should be amended as necessary, with customer agreement, to reflect changes in working practices, extra equipment, hours of cover etc.

SLAs relating to local IT equipment are particularly subject to changes in business requirement, equipment performance etc. Reviews should therefore be more, rather than less, frequent than for mainframe-based IT services. Where the IT directorate is acting as auditor or arbiter in a local SLA, attention should be given to the continued achievement of value for money from the service, with requests for improvements from customers being balanced against increased cost incurred by the customer.

5.1.6 Procurement policy

An efficient central procurement service, delivering the right goods at the right time with adequate customer support, is a major selling point in favour of retaining central IT control over local processors and terminals. On the other hand an inefficient central procurement service is a major source of discontent among customer management, who see central bureaucracy as obstructing the business function. It is therefore vital that this function is regularly audited for efficiency. Its customers should be questioned about the perceived efficiency, since this may not necessarily concur with statistics collected by the procurement function itself.

Quantitative measures could be used to evaluate the success of the procurement policy. These metrics could include:

* the percentage of PCs bought through central budget as opposed to local petty cash procurements

* the percentage of procurements that were deemed to be outside the policy

The IT Infrastructure Library
Management of Local Processors and Terminals

* the number of procurements completed within the customer's timescale.

Published results from a customer satisfaction questionnaire, sent to customers two months after installation would also produce metrics. These will be more subjective but will nonetheless be a valuable indication of success or failure.

Reviews should ensure that all appropriate legislative requirements have been complied with, including EC/GATT obligations where appropriate.

5.1.7 Support

Customer satisfaction with the quality of support services from the IT directorate should be monitored on an ongoing basis by the LSAs.

The production and revision of documentation should be reviewed in the light of feedback and customer needs. Checks should be made to ensure that the documentation is available at the point of use.

Regular surveys of the customer base should be aimed at refining the quality of support given by the MLPT. The results could be used as part of the training programme for LSAs, MLPT and Help Desk staff. Real life examples can be used as case studies for course exercises in customer care or technical support.

Regular review of the contents of the LITES manual, issuing updates and amendments as required is essential. Check that the guide is held by all customer areas and that all end-users have access to it. Seek views from LSAs and customers as to the manual's relevance, ease of use and accuracy.

5.1.8 Training

Training courses should be evaluated in the terms of relevance to business needs; specialist courses may be tailorable to meet evolving needs and to maximize value.

Course reviews (carried out at the end of the course and again after, say, three months) should confirm (or deny) training effectiveness and surveys should be carried out to determine the need for follow-up or refresher training.

The IT directorate might advise on the use of self-teach and computer-based training systems, possibly providing hardware and facilities for such training.

Section 5
Post-implementation and audit

5.1.9 Configuration management

Configuration audits should be carried out as advised in the **Configuration Management** module.

The MLPT, through the LSAs, should periodically check the whereabouts and usage of local processors and terminals. This check should span equipment:

* used in offices throughout the organization
* kept as backup in storage area in the customer domain
* used for home working
* used within the IT directorate for
    - development of software for local processors
    - simulation of customer systems by Help Desk and problem management staff
    - local processing.

The checks should determine if unauthorized modifications have been made, such as the installation of 'pirate' software.

Differences between the CMDB records and audit findings which occur frequently should be investigated. Such discrepancies could be open to interpretation as customers tailoring a system to their needs. In this case, encouragement should be given to customers to submit formal requests for change, rather than initiate their own *ad-hoc*, and possible harmful, alterations.

5.1.10 Capacity management

Monitor, as far as possible, the usage of the IT equipment sited in the customer domain. Assess the likely need for upgrades or the addition to the approved list of more (or less) powerful PCs. Especially monitor LAN and file server usage, aiming to recommend upgrades before any noticeable degradation in service occurs.

5.1.11 Software control and distribution

Any configuration management reviews undertaken by the LSAs should include software audits to ensure that the latest releases are being used and that unauthorized versions of software are not present.

The installation and acceptance reviews should include questions about the ease of software upgrades and whether automatic data conversions were available to ensure upward compatibility.

5.1.12 Installation, acceptance and testing

Customer satisfaction with installed equipment and procedures should be confirmed through interviews and/or questionnaires, and action plans agreed to overcome any deficiencies, liaising with the suppliers and installer (if different) as appropriate.

Configuration records on the CMDBs should be amended by LSAs to reflect any rejected hardware or software.

The MLPT should review the standards for product installation to ensure that the systems and procedures provided are as easy to use as anticipated and act upon feedback received from customers. The review should also ensure that installation is being carried out with ease of use as a priority. There is always a possibility that actual installations are carried out to minimize technical complication to the installer, rather than extra time and trouble being taken to provide the set-up that will best serve the customer in the long term.

The review should encompass all aspects of installation and acceptance testing (including customer support and training) to ensure that theintroduction of IT into the customer's working practice is fully evaluated.

The efficiency of the various service providers, in carrying out the installation of equipment and services should be reviewed.

5.1.13 Cost management

Review actual costs against any delegated budgets. Investigate wherever any costs for providing services to particular customers are significantly different from expectation. Check underspends with as much vigour as overspends, since these could be an indication of IT equipment being under utilized, possibly due to lack of customer awareness or confidence.

… Section 5
Post-implementation and audit

The MLPT should liaise with the cost manager who will require information to update financial forecasts in the light of workload forecasts, technological developments and SLA plans. This information will be used as input for the tactical infrastructure planning process, including the allocation of funds and resources.

5.1.14 Problem and change management

The problem management system should be reviewed to ensure that it provides the required service to customers of local processors and terminals. Problem management staff within IT Services must be aware of the degree of dependence of the business on local processing equipment.

The change management function should also be reviewed, with consideration given to the following:

* is formal change management causing an unacceptable delay to the introduction of changes needed to support business functions, especially consider

    - the cost of small changes against the delay

    - the frequency with which such changes are rejected or questioned by the CAB

    - the possibility of introducing or revising a cost threshold below which changes affecting a single customer department can be signed off by the business manager and change manager

* are approved changes being promulgated to all relevant local processors and terminals?

5.1.15 Security

Regular monitoring of the procedures specified in the security policy must be carried out by the IT security function with the co-operation of the LSAs. Changes in protective measures should be reviewed as a result of changes in configuration or sensitivity of data processed and agreed with all relevant parties.

Periodic checks should also be made as to the data integrity and security arrangements of all IT services on local processors. This may be combined with a configuration audit, or a review of building security. Working practices should be brought into line with new legislation or organizational codes of practice.

The IT Infrastructure Library
Management of Local Processors and Terminals

Security audits carried out by MLPT staff should include those areas, in terms of data, hardware and software, that have been made the responsibility of customers or customer management. Dependent upon the organization's practices, liaison may be required with internal audit sections, IT security staff and the organization's security officer.

5.1.16 Auditing of procedures

In many organizations, local processors and terminals will have a wide geographical distribution. In all organizations they are likely to be distributed around various departments and differing operational directorates. This will inevitably lead to differences of control and security attitudes. In this situation the need for regular and thorough audits to be carried out by the IT directorate becomes essential if a consistent approach to IT is to be maintained by the organization.

.1 Purpose and scope of audits

Audits will be useful towards the following:

* detecting and minimizing the loss or unauthorized movement of assets

* monitoring the condition of installed hardware, and determining any factors, either environmental or customer-related, which may affect its usability

* determining the use and usage of local processing systems, and the continued justification for their retention by customers

* verifying if the configuration and capacity of IT systems provide sufficient performance to meet local needs

* maintaining information and data security, and compliance with copyright and data protection legislation

* assessing the success of the IT directorate both in getting its messages across to customers, and in effecting action

* informally gauging customer satisfaction with support and facilities provided by the IT directorate and LSAs.

Section 5
Post-implementation and audit

.2 Implementing audits

The distributed nature and possible numbers of local IT systems raises the following practical issues:

* in a dynamic and fast-changing environment, the implementation timescale will have to be planned so that the snapshot of practice will be usable and not appreciably out-of-date (the unit responsible for audit must keep especially aware of developments within the customer domain during the course of the exercise)

* the dispersal of equipment may make it beneficial for various audits to be performed on one visit

* the complexity of some systems will require the use of suitably experienced staff, who may need to be released from other duties

* the sensitive nature of data on some services or work being carried out in some locations may make the involvement of outside parties, even from the same organization, undesirable

* some equipment may be in use by mobile or absent staff, at home addresses or the premises of maintenance agents, and therefore require special consideration

* the audits will inevitably involve some disruption to customers' usual work, and should be carried out with due planning, notice and publicity, including the endorsement of senior management

* as implied blame may be felt, the audits must be sensitively carried out with regards to staff morale and industrial relations, but without compromising any essentials (interpersonal skills will be an important factor in the selection of staff to carry out the audits)

* careful consideration must be given by management to the use of escalation procedures in the event of non co-operation and sanctions in the event of misconduct (it may be judicious to delay announcing follow-up actions on the latter until the size of the problem is accurately known)

* the effort involved should be commensurate with the benefits it is hoped will be achieved; both should be clearly measurable to allow the effectiveness of the audit to be evaluated

* the volume of data to be amassed and checked could be very large, however the effort of collation may be reduced by the appropriate use of pre-printed forms and automated tools

* in some circumstances, it may be possible for the co-operation of experienced customers and system administrators to be sought in completing returns in response to a questionnaire, although at least a sample of the data should still be verified directly

* special provision may be needed to test out some aspects of operations, such as the ability of fallback processing and/or procedures to be brought into use, or the ability to reload and verify archived data

* audits may encompass working practices, such as the review of backup, cleaning and other maintenance records, as well as the inspection of processing hardware.

.3 **Follow-up action**

Any discrepancies between actual and expected use should be investigated, and action plans drawn up to recommend corrective action.

5.2 Dependencies

The key dependencies in post-implementation review and audit are the knowledge gathering skills and procedures of reviewers and auditors.

The amount of time and effort involved in performing audit activities should not be underestimated especially in the case of widely dispersed IT systems.

It is important that the LSAs and the other support staff in IT Services are given the opportunity to express their views on the services offered to customers. These should be compared with customers' views and discrepancies addressed. Formal and informal meetings can yield good ideas and suggestions on improvements to customer services, helping to co-ordinate the service-oriented approach that is required across the IT directorate.

5.3 People

A review should be held to establish:

* the staff, both from the IT directorate and customer domain, actually involved in the various supporting functions

- whether the existing organizational structure facilitates their involvement, or if improvements or streamlining could be initiated
- the number of staff and appropriate skill levels required to support the functions identified as necessary
- the training required by staff to continue, or improve, the service provided to customers.

Regular meetings between the MLPT and customers are vital if the agreed structure and division of management responsibilities is to function effectively.

In order to broaden the appropriate knowledge and skills of staff in this area it may be constructive to arrange staff rotation, attachments or exchanges between Help Desk staff and LSAs.

It is important due to the logical and physical separation of the staff involved in managing local processors and terminals, for the MLPT to instigate and maintain contacts with customers, Trades Union representatives, accommodation managers etc.

Consideration should be given to the retention of any local liaison staff, especially those appointed to help with the introduction of new applications.

It may be practical, in terms of efficient use of resources and as sources of broadening staff skills and knowledge, to use LSAs to carry out compliance audits of procedures in each others' areas of work.

5.4 Timing

Reviews on efficiency and effectiveness should be carried out regularly, as should forecasts on future workload and work patterns. In most organizations, audits on inventories and compliance to standards will be carried out annually. Where an organization is using a Quality Management System (QMS), these reviews will be specified within the QMS documentation.

The Help Desk could be used to drive the other review processes. Its own management information measures should be produced each month and these can be used to indicate the general health of the service offered to customers.

It should be remembered that some reviews are disruptive to the customer's work and an endless succession of questionnaires and surveys will quickly annoy participants and affect the quality of any results. It is advised that no more than two questionnaires should be sent out each year to any individual customer.

Section 6
Benefits, costs and possible problems

6. Benefits, costs and possible problems

This section details the benefits, costs and possible problems associated with central IT management adopting and maintaining a policy of co-ordination and control over local processors and terminals based on the guidance contained in this module.

6.1 Benefits

The introduction of the MLPT function will reduce the associated 'cost of quality' relating to the use of IT equipment in the customer domain. This is the cost to an organization, in terms of finance and resources, directly attributable to the absence of an appropriate quality management system. Introducing the function will help to increase the effectiveness and efficiency of the organization by:

* ensuring, as far as possible, that local processors are compatible with other local equipment, central IT systems, customer's and supplier's systems, increasing the ability of business areas to communicate with each other and thereby opening up new business opportunities and increasing corporate flexibility

* ensuring enough infrastructure of the right type is in the right place at the right time and is working satisfactorily thereby increasing customer productivity

* generating savings from central purchasing, maintenance etc

* introducing effective software control and distribution throughout local IT services, thereby assisting organizations to ensure they comply with relevant software licence requirements and offering considerable protection against malicious software

* identifying fall back facilities through a central co-ordinated control

* increasing the flexibility of staff, within and between business communities and IT directorate, by developing a common base of skills and knowledge throughout the organization

* identifying under-utilized or surplus equipment or resources

* improving resilience provision
* reducing the diversification of incidents within local IT services and easing the identification of underlying problems
* bringing all IT assets under control, by customer or MLPT as appropriate, through procedures tailored to meet local needs
* improving communication and business synergy between the customers and their IT service providers.

Where the recommendations on adopting SLAs are implemented, benefits will include:

* clearly defined availability and response projections allowing better planning by all involved parties; customers, Local Systems Administrators and IT directorate staff
* protection against unplanned change by the provision of a framework for measured change
* a guaranteed commitment to providing facilities
* a reduction in misunderstandings between IT service providers and their customers through clear documentation and objective measurement.

Where it is the intention in the future to transfer day-to-day control of IT services to customers, the existence of comprehensive documentation to a common standard will facilitate this.

6.2 Costs

Introducing a structured system of managing local processors and terminals brings with it some associated costs. The organization as a whole will find that these costs are more than compensated for by the consequent increase in business efficiency. Organizations who do nothing to co-ordinate the local processors and terminals in the customer domain will find the associated 'cost of quality' to be much higher than those costs associated with introducing the function. These other costs include:

* extra staff resources in the central IT directorate, needed to exercise central co-ordination
* additional overheads, such as travelling and subsistence, due to increased attendance at customer sites for meetings and audits

Section 6
Benefits, costs and possible problems

* documentation, publicity campaigns and newsletters
* costs of any support tools used.

Costs are also incurred due to the extra time needed to carry out properly the functions of co-ordinated central control including:

* negotiation of SLAs and subsequent reviews
* carrying out compliance, configuration and security audits and the management costs of effectiveness reviews
* consultation and regular meetings with trades unions, customer management etc
* centrally investigating future options and forward compatibility to be able to advise and guide customers in the choice of equipment, packages and training.

6.3 Possible problems

The major possible problem is the resistance from customer managers to change caused by the greater involvement in the management of local equipment by central IT staff. These problems can to a large extent be circumvented by explaining the significant business benefits which will accrue as a result of the introduction of the changes.

The temptation to apply formal and complex procedures designed to support a large mainframe IT service could lead to cumbersome practices, restricting the best use of small local computers. Pragmatism should be applied to adopt practices used elsewhere in an organization to support and enhance the business rather than to restrict it.

The IT Infrastructure Library
Management of Local Processors and Terminals

Section 7
Tools

7. Tools

No specific tools are envisaged as necessary for the management of local processors and terminals. A central IT directorate following the recommendations of the **IT Infrastructure Library** will be using tools which are suitable for the management of local processors and terminals, ie tools for incident and error control and for the configuration management database. These should encompass the local equipment and incidents and the MLPT and LSAs will require access to them. Access will also be required to tools used by the network management function, since local processors and terminals form, in effect, intercommunicating entities with networks.

Where configuration management is not practised in the organization or is not extended to cover equipment controlled by customers then an asset register detailing the type and location of all IT equipment, software and documentation in the customer domain and individual responsibilities must be held. This register will most easily be maintained and updated if it is held electronically. Cross references to relevant documentation for each installation should also be retained.

Tools designed to solve the problems associated with monitoring and updating the software on a widely distributed network of PCs exist. These will automatically distribute new and/or changed software to all of an organization's PCs, at the same time checking each of them for the presence of viruses, pirate software and also checking disk utilization.

A specialist software tool (Synchrony) for updating software and data on remote PCs from a host IBM machine is in widespread use, helping to ensure consistency throughout distributions of thousands of PCs in an organization.

The IT Infrastructure Library
Management of Local Processors and Terminals

8. Bibliography

CCTA IS Guide D1: Small Systems (ISBN 0 471 92541 1), John Wiley and Sons Ltd, 1989.

CCTA IS Guide D2: Microcomputer Systems and Software (ISBN 0 471 92542 X), John Wiley and Sons Ltd, 1989.

CCTA IS Guide D3: Office System Facilities (ISBN 0 471 92543 8), John Wiley and Sons Ltd, 1989.

Annex A   Glossary of Terms

Acronyms and abbreviations used in this module

CAB	Change Advisory Board
CBT	Computer based training
CCTA	The Government Centre for Information Systems
CI	Configuration Item
CMDB	Configuration Management DataBase
DIP	Dual In-line Packages
IC	Information Centre
IS	Information Systems
IT	Information Technology
ITSO	Information Technology Security Officer
LAN	Local Area Network
LITES	Local IT Equipment and Services
LSA	Local Systems Administrator
MLPT	Manager for Local Processors and Terminals
PC	Personal Computer
PRINCE	PRojects In Controlled Environments
QMS	Quality Management System
RFC	Request For Change
SLA	Service Level Agreement
SLM	Service Level Management
SSG	Small Systems Group
VDU	Visual Display Unit
WAN	Wide Area Network

The IT Infrastructure Library
Management of Local Processors and Terminals

Definitions used in this module

Configuration Item	A component of an IT Infrastructure, normally the smallest item that can changed independently of other components. Configuration Items may vary widely in complexity, size and type, from an entire system (including all hardware, software and documentation) to a single program module or minor hardware component.
Configuration management	The process of identifying and defining the configuration items in a system, recording and reporting the status of configuration items and requests for change, and verifying the completeness and correctness of configuration items.
Customer domain	A logical means of dividing the overall IT Infrastructure into components of related functionality. There are three physical domains - mainframe, network and customer. The customer domain covers terminals and local processors to which end-users have everyday physical access and over which they have some degree of direct control. *In practice in this module, it can be taken to mean* All areas of an organization which use IT services, excluding the IT directorate.
DIP switches	Configurable switches within a piece of IT equipment which will cause the equipment to function in specific ways.
Hacking	Intentional unauthorized access, actual or attempted, to a computer program or data.
Help Desk	The central point of contact through which all customers should communicate with the IT directorate on a day-to-day basis.
Incident	A single occurrence of a deviation from the specification of an IT infrastructure component or an aspect of service.
Local Systems Administrator	The person responsible for the day to day control of IT equipment, and the services running on that equipment, sited within the customer domain. The Local Systems Administrator will usually be a member of the business community, looking to the IT directorate for technical support.
Lead time	The period of time elapsing between placing an order for goods or services and their delivery.

Annex A
Glossary of terms

Manager for Local Processors and Terminals	The manager within the IT directorate responsible for the co-ordination of IT services based upon equipment sited within the customer domain.
Mirror disk	A computer system where all data is recorded simultaneously on two disk drives to provide non-stop operation should one fail.
Virus	Software code written with the intention of unofficial entry into other systems by means of covert propagation.

Annex B Example Service Level Agreement

This annex contains a sample Service Level Agreement (SLA) for use within the customer domain. Such SLAs are drawn up between the Local Systems Administrator (LSA), who is responsible for the day to day operation of the IT services running on local IT equipment, and the staff using those services in support of their daily work. It must be borne in mind that SLAs are not designed to be contractual documents and the benefits of applying an SLA will be realised even where the Local Systems Administrator is line-managed within the business community being supported.

SLAs identify responsibilities on both parties and this must be recognized.

B.1 Service Level Agreement - local network

For example purposes, this Service Level Agreement demonstrates merely the type of agreement possible between the parties involved in supplying a fairly complex file server based network throughout a business section. The example is not meant to be exhaustive in its coverage or totally realistic in its detail.

The service is supplied to Section N1, part of a organization's department N. An electronic mail service is available throughout the organization, this is under the direct control of the IT directorate, and subject to a separate Service Level Agreement. Included with any such SLA will be agreed lists:

* of all the supported hardware, software and documentation

* detailing the underpinning and associated agreements and contracts, including SLAs for E-mail and management information service, maintenance contracts with suppliers.

The IT Infrastructure Library
Management of Local Processors and Terminals

B.1.1 Example Service Level Agreement

1. **This Service Level Agreement is between**

    1.1 Direct business staff in Section *N1*

    1.2 Local Systems Administrator (LSA), Department *N*.

2. **The agreement is for the support of**

    a PC Network available in Section *N1*, with links to other networks in Department *N* for management information purposes, and throughout the organization for electronic mail. A full listing of supported hardware, software and documentation is at section 7 of this agreement. Section 8 provides details of associated agreements and contracts.

3. **Agreed facilities and workloads**

    3.1 The LSA undertakes to provide attended operation between 09:00 and 17:30 on normal working days, ie Monday-Friday, excluding Public Holidays. Unattended operation will usually be available between 17:40 and 09:00 on normal days and all day on other days.

    3.2 Section heads within Department *N1* undertake to notify LSA should workload exceed the agreed levels (see section 6) by more than 10% over a working day. Any requirement for overtime working will be communicated to the LSA not less than three working days beforehand.

    3.3 Users will address incidents, complaints and observations relating to all IT services to the LSA. Notwithstanding this normal procedure, users will maintain a right of direct access to the IT directorate's central Help Desk facility.

4. **Terms of support**

    Local Systems Administrator Responsibilities (in any rolling 2 week period):

    4.1 To ensure that central processing facilities for applications *AA* and *PP* are available for 98% of the working days. As a system backup will be taken between 13:30 and 14:00 each working day, the facility for update access to the database *AA* will be available 95%.

Annex B
Example Service Level Agreement

4.2 To ensure that x PC workstations are available for 97% of the working days and x-2 workstations 98%.

Draft quality printers will be available 98% of the working days, and letter quality printers 96% with permitted additional downtime of 2 hours per 20,000 sheets printed.

4.3 In the event of contention for workstations, LSA will adjudicate on priority for access, which will normally favour *agreed priority users*.

4.4 LSA will maintain the speed of response at 3 seconds for queries on the *AA* database and 5 seconds for update transactions.

4.5 LSA will advise users of any factors affecting the availability or speed of response of the system.

4.6 LSA will advise users as to who the acting/cover administrators are at any given time.

4.7 LSA will liaise with the Premises Manager, Network Manager and the IT directorate over any scheduled events likely to affect the availability or response of the system, and provide at least 48 hours advance notice for any predictable loss of service greater than 30 minutes.

4.8 LSA will monitor all supporting service level agreements and contracts and liaise with the IT directorate and suppliers as appropriate.

4.9 LSA will act as the internal point of contact for any enquires by customers on the system, and log and progress any incident reports.

4.10 LSA will act as point of contact for any maintenance visits and sign-off callout paperwork as appropriate.

4.11 LSA will maintain a store of customer manuals and other system documentation such as records of serial numbers, configuration and changes implemented.

4.12 LSA will acknowledge written requests for new facilities or changes within 5 working days of receipt, and be responsible for forwarding such requests to change management staff.

4.13 LSA will keep the administration password(s), manuals and processor secure to prevent unauthorized access. All equipment under direct LSA control will be maintained in accordance with the Local IT Equipment and Services (LITES) manual.

4.14 LSA will provide one backup of all the data on the processor weekly and one backup daily if only the data is changed. Separate backups will be taken depending upon the value of data (to be agreed by the parties involved) or the installation of new facilities. All backup tapes will be stored in a fireproof safe on site, with duplicate copies of each tape stored off site.

5. User responsibilities

5.1 N1 undertake not to delete or modify installed files on their PC, or not to install any separate software/hardware on networked resources (including PCs) save with the consent of LSA.

5.2 N1 undertake to raise any problems in use with LSA as soon as they arise. In the absence of LSA, the IT Help Desk should be contacted.

5.3 N1 will inform LSA of any changes in use which might affect the network's registration under Data Protection legislation and/or the terms of the SLA.

5.4 N1 will not move the PC, save with the consent of LSA.

5.5 N1 will maintain their working environment in line with the LITES manual.

5.6 N1 undertake not to handle the central processor, system printers or cabling except with the agreement of LSA.

5.7 N1 will not leave their PCs in such a way that others may access personal or corporate data on a network when unattended, and will keep their network passwords secure.

5.8 N1 will keep secure copies of any programs or data which need to be taken outside of official backups.

5.9 N1 will delete user files when not required.

Annex B
Example Service Level Agreement

6. **Agreed workloads for Department N are as detailed below:**

   This section will contain the workload patterns anticipated for the duration of the SLA. The LSA's planning, including ordering of consumables, preventative maintenance will be based upon this information.

7. **Supported hardware, software and documentation**

   This section will contain an exhaustive list of the hardware and software pertaining to the SLA. It will also cover all relevant documentation relating to the equipment and services concerned. This section will also detail responsibilities for maintaining the documentation.

8. **Associated agreements and contracts.**

   This section will detail all agreements and contracts upon which the SLA depends including:

   * SLAs between IT directorate and the general customer community covering such services as:
     - Help Desk
     - E-mail
     - change management
     - contingency and maintenance
   * maintenance contracts with external suppliers and/or maintenance firms
   * agreements with telecommunications suppliers
   * contracts with suppliers for consumables, air-conditioning, electricity etc.

9. Signatories and validity

This agreement has been accepted by the undersigned as defining the terms of supply of the IT services detailed in section 7 above. It is valid for a period of 12 months from *(agreed starting date)*

Signed _____ - for users

_____ - Local Systems Administrator

(The MLPT should also sign this document to demonstrate that it had been audited and was in accordance with the IT directorate's policies relating to SLAs.)

Annex C Acceptance, testing and installation

C.1 General considerations

The acceptance, testing and installation of local processors and terminals falls into two different areas. Firstly, as with large scale IT installations, technical and compatibility aspects must be considered, ie new hardware, software and documentation must be subject to rigorous acceptance testing to ensure that it is complete and performing to the required specifications. Additionally, with local processing installations, this hardware, software and documentation must be delivered, ie installed into multiple customer locations.

These two aspects have differing considerations and should be addressed separately. In particular, no attempts should be made to install hardware or software into the customer domain until it has been shown to work satisfactorily under test in the IT directorate.

C.2 Technical acceptance standards

For installations to be carried out in a consistent and thorough manner, detailed and comprehensive installation standards must be documented.

It is advisable that this process be carried out by the IT directorate, or at least managed by them, where components are purchased part-installed from dealers or other sources.

Once agreed the standards may be copied to parties such as local systems administration, Help Desk, maintenance providers and equipment suppliers, or used, as far as is possible, for automating the installation process.

C.2.1 Compatibility standards

To recommend, supply or support local processing systems effectively, IT directorate must adopt technically appropriate and consistent product standards. Some of the more common points to watch for include:

* compatibility between different versions of the same package, and any data files used. (There may be 100% backward compatibility, alternatively a conversion program may have to be used)

The IT Infrastructure Library
Management of Local Processors and Terminals

* compatibility between packages and the operating system

* 'well behaved' packages should be portable between current and subsequent versions of the same operating system on a particular machine, but those which access hardware directly may fail to be portable across versions or machines. This may be due to reasons of capacity (eg memory required) or dependence upon a particular configuration of the operating system

* compatibility between different packages in the same environment

    - if packages cannot exchange data in a mutually acceptable format, (eg TIFF, ASCII), a data conversion utility may need to be purchased

    - different packages may fail to work concurrently, due to conflicting demands upon machine resources, most typically memory, but also where they use different device drivers or ports (eg a serial port for a mouse). Colour and keyboard operations may be noticeably affected

    - communications packages may load a particular keyboard driver resulting in problems, eg when using shortcut commands within an application expecting a different configuration

    - when additional cards are loaded into processors, care should be taken to prevent interrupt line and memory address conflicts between applications

* some applications may work in some circumstances only in a given environment

    - for instance, a PC application may work on a PC only when a PC operating system is loaded, not a network operating system

    - alternatively, a PC application may be able to use a network printer or hard disk, but not operate in a multi-customer mode with file-locking

    - some packages will work in a windowing environment in 'full screen mode', but have not been specifically written to take advantage of all the environment's facilities such as data exchange or split screen operation.

Annex C
Acceptance, testing and installation

If the organization has not already developed a policy on a common user interface approach, this should be considered as a means of improving usability. Consistency of user interface between packages and their conformance with the organization's policy should be taken into consideration.

C.2.2 Installation standards

Once a suitable range of supported software and compatibility rules have been established, the derivation and adoption of installation standards will simplify the delivery and final process, simplifying the development of installation scripts (simple to follow step-by-step guidance on the installation of IT hardware and/or software). The scope of these standards will include:

* tailoring the customer interface to shield the customer from unnecessary complexity and protect the computer from potential misuse

* providing help and/or self-tuition facilities for applications

* establishing suitable defaults, ideally this would be done consistently across packages, although this is not always possible with software of different origins. It is necessary to involve customer representatives in the selection and tailoring of packages eg

    - screen colour
    - use of particular character sets/fonts
    - screen resolution
    - operation of function keys
    - use of audible alerts
    - cursor characteristics
    - use of particular stationery in output devices

* defining an efficient and secure machine environment, eg

    - meaningful directory and path names
    - hiding/protecting system files
    - implementing suitable operating system defaults, such as for time slicing and buffering

- tailoring customer access profiles on a 'need to use' basis

* ensuring software is installed legally

* automating the installation of commonly used parameter and data files to save time and ensure consistency

* levels of sign-off required from installation, customer and (possibly) supplier staff.

Each new installation will require a workstation analysis to comply with health and safety requirements. In the UK these are contained within the Health and Safety at Work etc Act, which incorporates the EC directive on Display Screen Equipment.

C.3 Delivery considerations

As well as arranging for the physical installation of hardware and software and verifying that the required functions are supported, the delivery process must, wherever possible, also ensure:

* the customer site is adequately set to support the delivered equipment ie

    - environmental considerations are satisfactory, eg temperature control, cabling considerations

    - interfaces with the supported business functions are in place

    - sufficient suitably trained staff are available

* equipment is clearly marked, where necessary with

    - model and serial numbers

    - security markings, to deter theft

    - Help Desk contact numbers

    - warning markers eg fragile, hot parts, electrical risk

* all relevant documentation is supplied eg

    - manufacturers' manuals

    - LITES manual

    - keyboard templates

Annex C
Acceptance, testing and installation

- check lists such as back up calendars
- paperwork to record acceptance by customer of responsibility for delivered items.

C.3.1 Delivery options

Since local processing equipment is sited within the customer domain, IT directorate management will have to make conscious decisions about the policy for installation and checking of new and repaired equipment. Several broad options are possible including:

* central delivery to IT directorate accommodation with checking by IT directorate staff
* direct delivery to customer premises, either with or without attendance by IT directorate staff.

There are several influencing factors to take into account when deciding on the best policy for a particular organization and situation viz:

* time allowed by supplier to register faults in supplied equipment
* physical separation between IT directorate and customer premises, including accessibility
* size, portability and fragility of the equipment in question
* importance of the business function supported
* knowledge and reliability of both local administration staff and suppliers
* whether equipment is being installed by suppliers or merely delivered by transport firm
* familiarity of IT directorate staff with the installation and set-up requirements of the delivered equipment
* availability of standard performance and compliance checks and the degree of knowledge and skill required to carry them out.

.1 Central delivery

This is most appropriate for reasonably small, expensive and easily transported equipment, especially where there is a short fault registering period and a fairly high level of initial testing is felt to be necessary. A major consideration is the final geographical distribution of the equipment.

Central delivery is an attractive prospect in a single large headquarters building with several customer departments collocated with the IT directorate. It is much less attractive for an organization with a central IT directorate and customer sites distributed around the country. Benefits include:

* the consistent and thorough checking of equipment
* reduced costs made possible by a single central receipt point and/or by bulk purchasing
* installation at the customer site by IT directorate staff which allows
    - the opportunity for extra customer training and additional support from IT directorate
    - encourages IT directorate staff to keep in touch with the customers
* quicker rectification of possible problems
* the possibility of establishing a central pool of popular equipment to speed up the procurement and installation process.

Disadvantages can include:

* the risk of transport damage on a second move from IT directorate to customer
* increased expense in IT directorate staff resources and accommodation requirements centrally
* it may be impractical for large equipment.

.2 **Direct delivery with IT directorate staff present**

This method is most practical for complicated, high value and high profile equipment. Typically complicated installations such as mini computers or LANs might have an IT directorate presence extending over several days. Alternatively initial deliveries of equipment new to the organization, eg first delivery of a new standard PC or printer may warrant IT directorate attendance. Advantages of this approach include:

* single delivery of equipment, at supplier's risk
* IT directorate staff keep in touch with customers
* it allows assessment of installation standards and support provided by supplier.

Annex C
Acceptance, testing and installation

Disadvantages include the cost of IT directorate staff time and expenses.

.3 Direct delivery with no IT directorate presence

This is generally used for uncomplicated equipment especially where it can be plugged in with minimal setting up, eg printers. It can also be viable where the known level of supplier support is good and/or where skilled and trusted customer staff are available. The advantages include:

* it is the cheapest option

* single delivery of equipment is at the suppliers risk.

Disadvantages include:

* the possibility of a lack of consistency in set-up parameters for identical equipment in different locations, reducing portability benefits

* it could enable unapproved software to be installed which could result in
    - a breach of software licence conditions
    - the introduction of malicious software

* that customer staff are more likely to feel that they are the owners of the new equipment and less likely to acknowledge any degree of IT directorate control over it.

In practice most organizations will use a mix of these options for different equipment and for different customers, depending on the degree of skill available in the specific customer area or required by the specific equipment in question. IT directorate staff should attend occasional installations by suppliers to assess and monitor the degree and quality of support being provided.

Whichever procedure is used in any given situation, relevant paperwork must be developed to support the information flows required. In particular, notification to customers before installation, relevant installation instruction and/or software, and return confirmation paperwork must be in use. Normally this communication would be routed via the Help Desk.

The IT Infrastructure Library
Management of Local Processors and Terminals

C.3.2 Installation & checking of delivered items

Whoever is chosen to carry out the initial inspection of newly delivered items, there is much to be gained by providing a standard script to ensure that all equipment is subject to the same level and scope of inspection and testing. These check lists should cover all the salient points of the installation and inspection including:

* correct items delivered to correct location
* physical inspection for damage
* verification of serial numbers and model types
* verification of facilities and functions expected
* confirmation of any installation support required
* confirmation of any registrations required eg for guarantee purposes
* confirmation of compatibility with other equipment/ software etc
* completion of all associated paperwork including
    - registration of guarantees
    - notification to Help Desk of successful installation
    - affixing of templates, help stickers, configuration item descriptions.

Such a script for installation and inspection can vary from a chatty document, aimed at end users who are installing delivered kit, to a complicated test pattern to be run by skilled IT staff. In either case it serves several purposes in that it:

* ensures all staff receipt and test all equipment in a consistent fashion, thereby strengthening the validity of failure and problem statistics
* helps less skilled staff to cope and therefore saves resources
* allows suppliers and Help Desk staff to be aware of procedures and assists diagnosis in a telephone 'talk through' when problems arise

Annex C
Acceptance, testing and installation

* ensures systems are established in a standard fashion, again assisting Help Desk and other support staff and permitting greater staff portability.

An established standard practice for the installation of equipment will require the flexibility to cope with minor variations. For example, in a PC installation the specific script must be tailorable to reflect the different options available to customers. These might include:

* colour or monochrome monitor
* size and number of disk drives
* speed, capacity and capabilities of supplied printer
* specific applications supplied
* use of mouse or similar facilities.

The script need not be constrained to a single medium, all scripts will require some element of paper based instruction but much of the script can be produced in software supplied either with the equipment, or in advance from the IT directorate, usually via the Help Desk. Where for example a new PC installation is taking place, the software can be supplied together with batch files to set up the disks, load on copies of proprietary and in house packages, initiate links to networks and upload files etc. All this can be done together with meaningful messages supplied to staff carrying out the installation, instructing them on which disks to load etc.

C.4 Example script for receipt, checking & installing a PC

A simplified example of a typical checklist for the receipt, checking, installation and acceptance of a 'standard' PC is given here by way of illustration.

1. Ensure the number of packages received agrees with the delivery paperwork and that items are addressed to the expected recipient.

2. Check that the items on the delivery note agree with:

    * advance paperwork eg order forms, advice notes
    * labelling on packages.

Note: Should any discrepancies be identified between the paperwork and delivered items please contact Help Desk before opening boxes.

The IT Infrastructure Library
Management of Local Processors and Terminals

3. Unpack all boxes and arrange equipment in the working location. The following procedure is advised:

    * ensure chosen location has sufficient electrical outlets within reach and there is adequate room for all the equipment concerned

    * construct printer stand first, place stand to side of PC table, unpack printer and place on stand

    * unpack processor, place on PC table, remove blank from floppy disk drive

    * construct tilt and swivel stand for monitor, open VDU box and place terminal upside down on floor, fix tilt and swivel stand to underside of terminal (following instructions supplied with the stand), lift whole assembly and place right way up in working position. Typically the terminal will be sited alongside or on top of the processor.

    Note: the terminal, especially if it is a colour terminal, is very heavy, it is recommended that this be lifted into position by 2 people.

4. Obtain all relevant cables from the boxes, connect processor, printer and terminal to the mains, connect processor-printer and processor-terminal cables, position keyboard and insert cable to rear of processor.

5. You will have received from the Help desk a set of floppy disks, insert the disk marked 'First Start Up' into the floppy disk drive, turn all equipment on at the mains and at the switches on the equipment itself.

6. The PC should now start itself up. The programs on the disk supplied will lead you through the rest of the initialization and testing process for your new PC. Contact the Help Desk on XXXXX if you need any assistance or if any piece of equipment fails to perform as predicted.

Annex D Skills and training required

D.1 Skills requirements

Staff involved in the management of local processors and terminals, whether working for the MLPT in the IT directorate or LSAs working in the customer domain will need to have a broad base of skills. Apart from the technical knowledge needed to support the agreed range of products, there will be the need to liaise with customers at all levels of seniority and expertise; and this will provide a test of interpersonal and communications skills.

The MLPT will need to have the same set of skills, plus the ability to direct and motivate their staff. The size of the installed base of services and the dynamic nature of the customers' business environment will require the abilities to gather and sift information, and handle potential conflict in establishing relative priorities across the organization.

A keen business awareness should be supplemented by the ability to understand developments and trends in Information Technology, and be able to relate the perspective to local plans of action.

A checklist is provided to cover the skills and knowledge that might typically be required:

* resource management
    - budget management
    - appreciation of accounting practice
    - project management
    - staff management and motivation
    - time management
    - forecasting
* interpersonal skills
    - understanding people
    - tact
    - patience
    - persuasiveness
    - negotiation skills
    - relationship building

* communication skills
  - good telephone manner
  - drafting ability
  - formal presentation skills
  - appreciation of graphics
  - being a good listener
  - non-verbal communications skills
* information handling skills
  - awareness of information gathering techniques
  - literacy
  - numeracy
  - ability to interpret statistics
  - analytical ability
  - decision making
  - maintenance of filing system or library
  - use of automated tools.

The reality of course, is that the chances of finding several people with all the above skills to populate the function controlling the management of local processors within an organization, are remote. In practice, when appointing staff, the skill points identified must be ranked in the light of the circumstances pertaining to the organization and specific posts concerned. This in turn requires that IT Services managers responsible for appointing staff to this rôle, must be aware of the organization in sufficient detail to make an informed decision about the suitability of candidates.

D.2 Training requirements

By law (Health & Safety at Work etc Act, Employment Protection Act, etc), organizations must train their staff to be able to perform their duties. Training should be provided, both vocationally (ie towards a specific business objective) and to enable staff to comply with health and safety regulations. The legal obligations refer only to the

Annex D
Skills and training required

minimum requirements for training. Expenditure on relevant training should be viewed as an investment which will more than repay itself in terms of increased effectiveness from well trained staff.

Organizations should adopt a policy on whether formal training should be provided before an employee is given access to a computer system. Such a decision will depend on the nature of data held and the level of risk. For instance it may be possible to let a clerk with some computer familiarity experiment with a spreadsheet or word-processing package on a stand-alone PC, but undesirable to let the same person have access to a corporate personnel records system.

Where staff need to be trained to use a transaction processing system, there may be options to use either a live service under supervision, or a parallel 'training system' which uses fictitious data. The IT directorate may be called upon to assist in setting up a training system or the use of externally developed computer based training (CBT) for the more popularly available packages.

Where staff (IT or customer) are responsible for a computer, such as network file server or mini-computer, it may be preferable to use a manufacturer's or manufacturer-accredited training course.

Whether or not quality audits are carried out, training records should be kept, and the trainee's employment history updated. In most organizations these records will be maintained as part of the personnel function. Where training is carried out on-the-job, for instance where formal training is not readily available, the training is less likely to be recorded and the MLPT may, if necessary, need to keep separate records.

All training should be followed up with an 'end of course review', any points of difficulty or omission noted, and a plan drawn up to consider remedial action and a follow-up review date.

D.3 Rôle descriptions

The remainder of this annex contains example rôle descriptions and work objectives for the appropriate aspects of the jobs of relevant staff. These descriptions are necessarily for guidance only and will require tailoring to the precise circumstances pertaining to an organization.

D.3.1 Manager with responsibility for local processors and terminals

Where an organization makes use of a Small Systems Group (SSG) or Information Centre (IC), many aspects of the work carried out by that unit will fall outside the scope of this module, for example systems analysis and program development in response to perceived business functions. This rôle description does not address itself to those aspects but covers the elements relevant to IT service management, whether the responsibility is vested in SSG, IC, in combination with other service management functions or there is sufficient local equipment to warrant a full time post.

Main Duties

1 Support users in the use and management of their local terminals and processors, in line with Service Level Agreements (SLAs).

2 Maintain day-to-day communications with users and other IT staff, and identify any factors which might affect the continued relevance or attainment of SLAs.

3 Advise users on the suitable use of IT services in addressing their business requirements, and the formulation of requests for procuring hardware, software and services in line with standards.

4 Maintain an awareness of relevant products and practices within the user environment, and provide the co-ordination necessary to ensure that services are controlled in a manner that is secure, cost-effective, and compliant with legal and industrial relations requirements.

5 Ensure that local systems comply with organization and system security policies and procedures, including:

* password mechanisms
* combating viruses
* authorized software.

6 Develop a perspective of both organizational directions and developments within the IT industry, so as to be able to assist in the formulation of business and communications IS strategies.

Annex D
Skills and training required

7   Recruit and develop an organization to meet the above accountabilities.

8   Act as technical manager for Local Systems Administrators including:

- assist customer departments with selection and appointment
- ensure technical training is supplied
- monitor the technical competence and performance of LSAs.

D.3.2 Local Systems Administrator

The Local Systems Administrator (LSA) rôle will be responsible for the IT equipment and services located within one or more business communities. This may involve equipment at one or more geographically separate locations. The rôle may constitute a full time post in a large business area or where several business areas are supported, eg a large and/or complex LAN in a sizeable headquarters office, but is more likely to be combined with other business responsibilities. The LSA will normally be a member of the business community, reporting to the manager of the business function supported by the IT services running on the local IT equipment. This normal line management will be supplemented by a technical management supervision exercised by the MLPT. It is therefore essential that the LSA element of job descriptions are formally agreed by both areas of management (especially the percentage of time expected to be spent on LSA duties) and that meetings and procedures are arranged to ensure fair and accurate staff reporting takes place.

Main Duties

1   Be responsible for the smooth running of the managed local IT services in keeping with Service Level Agreements (SLAs).

2   Protect the integrity of data relating to the supported services, taking backups as necessary and arranging for their secure storage, liaising with database co-ordinators as required.

3   Control access to programs and to data files and other machine resources to users on a basis of operational necessity.

4 Act as local co-ordination point for reporting incidents to the Help Desk. Report all such incidents to the central Help Desk, including those solved locally. Act as local investigator and fixer for problems referred from Help Desk.

5 Provide input to the change management process for relevant change requests. Liaise with users and other interested parties over implementing approved changes which will affect the range, performance, availability or ease of use of the facilities provided.

6 Act as the initial contact for users for advice on how to use the IT service or rectify problems. Carry out familiarization training for new users and following the introduction of changes to the service.

7 Liaise with providers on which the IT service depends, such as external network managers, operations controllers for other computer systems, premises managers and maintenance agents.

8 Liaise with users and management over the maintenance of an SLA which will continue to meet business needs.

9 Maintain configuration, performance and maintenance records.

IT Infrastructure Library
Management of Local Processors and Terminals

Comments Sheet

CCTA hopes that you find this book both useful and interesting. We will welcome your comments and suggestions for improving it.
Please use this form or a photocopy, and continue on a further sheet if needed.

From:

                Name

              Organization

                Address

               Telephone

COVERAGE
Does the material cover your needs?
If not, then what additional material would you like included.

CLARITY
Are there any points which are unclear?
If yes, please detail where and why.

ACCURACY
Please give details of any inaccuracies found.

If more space is required for these or other comments, please continue overleaf.

IT Infrastructure Library
Management of Local Processors and Terminals

Comments Sheet

OTHER COMMENTS

Return to: **IT Infrastructure Management Services**
CCTA,
Gildengate House
Upper Green Lane
NORWICH, NR3 1DW

Further information

Further information on the contents of this module can be obtained from:

IT Infrastructure Management Services
CCTA
Gildengate House
Upper Green Lane
NORWICH
NR3 1DW.

Telephone: 0603 694808
(GTN: 3014 4808)